Analytical Psychology

Routledge Classics contains the very best of Routledge publishing over the past century or so, books that have, by popular consent, become established as classics in their field. Drawing on a fantastic heritage of innovative writing published by Routledge and its associated imprints, this series makes available in attractive, affordable form some of the most important works of modern times.

For a complete list of titles visit
www.routledge.com/classics

Carl Gustav
Jung

Analytical Psychology

Its Theory and Practice
(The Tavistock Lectures)

With a foreword by Kevin Lu

 London and New York

These lectures were delivered in English in 1935 and were first published in Great Britain in 1968. First published in paperback by Routledge 1976

First published in Routledge Classics 2014
by Routledge
2 Park Square, Milton Park, Abingdon, Oxon OX14 4RN

and by Routledge
711 Third Avenue, New York, NY 10017

Routledge is an imprint of the Taylor & Francis Group, an informa business

British Library Cataloguing in Publication Data
A catalogue record for this book is available from the British Library

Library of Congress Cataloging in Publication Data
A catalog record for this book has been requested

ISBN: 978-0-415-73869-9 (pbk)
ISBN: 978-1-315-77220-2 (ebk)

Typeset in Joanna MT by RefineCatch Limited, Bungay, Suffolk

CONTENTS

LIST OF ILLUSTRATIONS

Editorial Note

C. G. Jung was invited by the Institute of Medical Psychology (Tavistock Clinic), Malet Place, London, at the instigation of Dr J. A. Hadfield, to give a series of five lectures, which he delivered September 30 to October 4, 1935. According to the 1935 report of the Institute, the Lectures when announced were not titled. The audience, of some two hundred, consisted chiefly of members of the medical profession. A stenographic record was taken of the lectures and the subsequent discussions; the transcript was edited by Mary Barker and Margaret Game, passed by Professor Jung, and printed by mimeograph for private distribution by the Analytical Psychology Club of London, in 1936, under the title 'Fundamental Psychological Conceptions: A Report of Five Lectures by C. G. Jung. . . .' The work has become widely known as 'The Tavistock Lectures' or 'The London Seminars'.

Passages from the Lectures were published in a French translation by Dr Roland Cahen in his edition of Jung's *L'Homme à la découverte de son âme* (Geneva, 1944; 6th edn., Paris, 1962), where the editor inserted them in a transcript of a series of seminars that Jung gave to the Société de Psychologie of Basel in 1934. Jung included much of the same material in both the London and Basel series as well as in lectures given in 1934 and 1935 at the Eidgenössische Technische Hochschule, Zürich.

For the present edition, only minor stylistic revisions have been made, by R. F. C. Hull, translator of the Collected Works of C. G. Jung, under the supervision of the Editors of the Collected Works. The bibliographical notes inserted by the original editors have been augmented (in square brackets); most of these refer to Jung's other writings particularly after 1935. In an appendix, biographical information is supplied about the participants in the discussion.

Grateful acknowledgement is made to Mrs Barker and Mrs Game, for their co-operation; to those living among the participants in the discussion who gave permission to reproduce their remarks; to Dr Roland Cahen; and to Mr Sidney Gray, present secretary of the Tavistock Institute of Medical Psychology, for his assistance. For advice in the preparation of the notes, the Editors are obliged to Joseph Campbell, J. Desmond Clark, Etienne Gilson, Norbert Guterman, Mrs Lilly Jung, E. Dale Saunders, and Mrs Ruth Spiegel.

PREFATORY NOTE TO THE ORIGINAL EDITION

This report of Professor Jung's Lectures to the Institute of Medical Psychology is edited under the auspices of the Analytical Psychology Club, London.

On the whole the report is verbatim, though it has been considered advisable to alter the construction of certain sentences with a view to avoiding any ambiguity of meaning. The editors can only hope that in making these minor changes they have not destroyed the very individual flavour of the Lectures.

In a few cases it was found impossible to ascertain the names of those taking part in the discussions, nor was it practicable to submit proofs of their questions to each of the speakers. For this deficiency and for any possible errors in the reporting of questions we offer our apology.

The stencils of the charts, diagrams, and drawings have been cut with Professor Jung's permission from the originals in his possession.[1]

Our thanks are due to the Institute of Medical Psychology not only for giving the Analytical Psychology Club permission to report the Lectures but also for facilitating the work in every way. To Miss Toni Wolff we would express our special gratitude for helping us with our task. Finally, and above all, we wish to thank Professor Jung for answering questions about difficult points and for passing the report in its final form.

MARY BARKER

MARGARET GAME

London, October 1935

NOTE

1   [For the present edition, the charts and diagrams have been re-executed, and photographs of the drawings (actually water-colours) have kindly been furnished by Dr E. A. Bennet.]

FOREWORD TO THE ROUTLEDGE CLASSICS EDITION
KEVIN LU

Jung made several trips to Britain throughout his lifetime. In 1913, he deliv-ered two papers in London: one to the Psycho-Medical Society on August 5th and one during the 17th International Congress of Medicine, held between August 6th and 12th (McGuire [ed.], 1974: 549). At the end of July 1914, Jung gave a lecture to the British Medical Association at a congress held in Aberdeen (Jung, 1961/1989a: 176). At the end of WWI, Jung was invited by the Royal Society of Medicine and the Society for Psychical Research to give three lectures in July 1919 (Bair, 2003: 304). Between July 30th and August 6th 1938, Jung participated in the 10th International Medical Congress for Psychotherapy held at Oxford, where he discussed his efforts to promote dialogue amongst the varying schools of psychotherapy (Hayman, 1999/2002: 359–60; Shamdasani, 2005–2006: 3–5). During this visit, he was awarded an honorary degree by the University of Oxford. Barbara Hannah recounts: 'A great many universities awarded honorary degrees on him [Jung], but the only time I remember Jung being at all excited by such an honour was at Oxford' (Hannah quoted in Shamdasani, 2005–2006: 3). Amongst those who congratulated Jung was a familiar face – Dr Hugh Crichton-Miller (Shamdasani, 2005–2006: 5).[1] Founder of the Tavistock Clinic, Crichton-Miller had chaired the first of five lectures Jung had given there three years earlier, in 1935, at the age of sixty.[2] Crichton-Miller was later to prove to be a close acquaintance and ally during one of the most turbulent periods in Jung's life when he was accused of anti-Semitism and collabora-tion with the Nazis, a period which was to cast a lasting shadow over his international reputation (Samuels, 1988).

Jung certainly made an indelible impression on the British medical profession when he visited London to deliver what are now widely known as either 'The Tavistock Lectures' or 'The London Seminars'. What is up for debate is whether that impression was favourable. In a climate in which psychoanalysis was 'all the rage' (Beckett quoted in Bair, 2003: 414), Deirdre Bair suggests that the overall consensus was a positive one, though she notes that Jung's questionable views on contemporary politics would have been known to some in the audience (ibid.: 416). As evidence of this positive reception by the predominantly British gathering, Bair indicates that the applause Jung received at the conclusion of the lectures 'was far more sustained than mere politeness required' (ibid.), an assessment based on the impressions of Joseph Henderson, Joseph Wheelright, E. A. Bennet, H. G. Baynes and Samuel Beckett, all present at the event. It is equally important and interesting to note that four of the five individuals cited by Bair were within Jung's inner circle, two of whom were American (Henderson and Wheelright). Samuel Beckett, as is widely known, attended the third lecture as a guest of his then analyst, W. R. Bion. Beckett was deeply affected by what Jung had to say and, arguably, analytical psychological concepts informed some of his later works (Bair, 2003: 414; Hinshelwood, 2013: 48; Campbell, 2005). Bair's representation of Jung's performance – in which he turned scepticism into 'acceptance and appreciation' (Bair, 2003: 416) – is largely drawn from accounts given by those with a vested interest in the advancement of analytical psychology. Bair supports her position by noting how Jung generously gave up his time, including early mornings and late evenings, for private conversations and therapeutic consultation (ibid.). Although Bair rightly notes that some tensions flared during discussions following the fourth lecture (ibid.: 414), there is little to suggest that the reception of the 'Tavistock Lectures' was anything but positive.

Sonu Shamdasani has, however, suggested the possibility of a different reaction to Jung's Tavistock Lectures. In his notes to a mimeographed edition of the lectures printed in 1936 and held at the Wellcome Library Archives in London, Shamdasani refers to a conversation he held with Michael Fordham in which Fordham, who had been present at the 1935 lectures, stated that the edition published for public consumption in 1968 was heavily revised. In particular, what was deemed to be Jung's 'rudeness' to the gathering of prominent British psychiatrists and psychologists was edited out. A comparison of the five discussions in the 1936 mimeographed edition and the published 1968 version unearthed no less than 277 modifications. These ranged from minor stylistic changes and deletions to more significant alterations (for instance, sentences omitted and others rewritten). A few of the changes are significant enough to prompt one to question Jung's intended meaning. However, my own study of the discussions did not unearth any such compelling variations intended to tone down Jung's rudeness; in my opinion Jung's 'rudeness' to his audience remains quite evident, despite the editorial changes. To all intents and purposes, then, accounts of the discussion periods remain the same. One cannot, however, dismiss the possibility that Jung's alleged disdain for his audience was mitigated by several editors: R. F. C. Hull, Mary Barker and Margaret Game. The very fact that at least 277 alterations exist brings into question the assertion that R. F. C. Hull made only 'minor stylistic revisions' (Jung, 1968: ix). A thorough comparison of extant versions of the text is certainly required. Shamdasani indicates that an involved correspondence arose concerning the editing of the text, especially around the question of whether Jung's words should be tempered. An equally comprehensive examination of Jung's correspondence, and that of his followers, is not only necessary but may unearth more details concerning the general reception of Jung in Britain.[3]

My decision to start with a comparison of the discussions was far from cursory. A major reason why the 'Tavistock Lectures' are important is because of the lively exchanges that followed each lecture. Although I was disturbed to discover the number of editorial changes made to the discussions, I was relieved that their general ethos and tone had been preserved (as far as we can tell at the time of writing). The questions posed to Jung forced him to clarify his own position and thinking, which at times could be both vague and controversial. At other points, the discussions offered Jung an opportunity to define key analytical psychological concepts (see Jung's definition of *active imagination* [1968: 190]). Here, we perhaps find Jung at his most lucid, providing detailed examples that crystallize his complex theories, thereby making them accessible to a wider public.

What is refreshing is that Jung's audience was not merely comprised of the converted, which meant that many were unafraid to challenge Jung on several points throughout his five lectures. The excitement born of the tension and atmosphere of intellectual debate is palpable; we get a sense that those in the room who participated in the discussions were passionate about their profession and that the profession itself was changing because of the important discoveries being made in the field. This brings me to another reason why the discussions are crucial to an understanding of analytical psychology – they force us to acknowledge that Jung's thinking cannot be divorced from its intellectual milieu. The people in the room specifically and the discussions more generally serve as keyholes through which we can glimpse the living context of psychology and medicine in which Jung's work was inevitably situated.

The general direction and identity of the Tavistock Clinic at the time help to explain why Jung was invited to deliver the lectures. The clinic's eclectic range of interests and general open-mindedness – described by Nuno Torres and Robert D. Hinshelwood as an 'integrative urge to bring biological, social and psychological studies of human beings together' (2013: 38) – provided Jung with the optimum environment and a timely platform to present his unique perspective and psychological theory as distinct from that of psychoanalysis. Hinshelwood describes the type of psychotherapy being practised at the Tavistock as 'a school of [. . .] its own, dedicated to a kind of integrative eclectic practice which included the ideas of Jung as well as Freud' (Hinshelwood, 2013: 45). The clinic's willingness to explore different depth psychological models even aroused the ire of Ernest Jones, who forbade psychoanalysts from working at the Tavistock (ibid.).

The Tavistock's broad-minded approach was nourished by its founder, Crichton-Miller, and two of his early associates, James Arthur Hadfield and Ian Dishart Suttie (Torres and Hinshelwood, 2013; Hinshelwood, 2013). All three were present at Jung's 'Tavistock Lectures' – Crichton-Miller and Hadfield served as chairs for the first and second lectures respectively, and Hadfield and Suttie participated in the discussions. The influence of Crichton-Miller and Hadfield on the profession was considerable, and their connection to Jung strong, which explains why Jung was their obvious choice to deliver the 1935 lectures.

Crichton-Miller, a practising psychotherapist before WWI, forwarded a doctrine of psychophysical parallelism to which Jung spoke in discussions one and two. The Tavistock grew out of Crichton-Miller's wartime experience with those suffering psychological difficulties as a consequence of the war, and much of his work centred on what he termed a 'binocular approach' – a 'psychophysical interactionist model [. . .] in which emotions, mental stability and physical factors [. . .] interacted via the endocrine and circulatory systems' (Torres and Hinshelwood, 2013: 37). Crichton-Miller was not, however, a psychoanalyst and held a non-partisan view of psychoanalysis, which inevitably shaped the Tavistock's relationship to the field. Although his resignation as Director in 1933 marked his declining influence, something of Crichton-Miller's integrative outlook persisted amongst the Tavistock staff (Hinshelwood, 2013: 46).

It is not unreasonable to suggest that Crichton-Miller's interests and eclectic approach to the psyche led Jung to consider him a friend. When Crichton-Miller died in 1959, Jung wrote a fond reflection of his impressions of the Tavistock's founder. When he first met Crichton-Miller, Jung recalls being 'deeply impressed by the friendly, open, and unprejudiced manner of his [Crichton-Miller's] welcome' (Jung, 1961/1989b: 639). Although the two held differing opinions, Jung felt that they 'were speaking the same language' and referred to Crichton-Miller as 'the only man of my age with whom I could talk as man to man, without constantly fearing that my partner would suddenly throw a fit or become otherwise impolite' (ibid.). Their supportive friendship would prove crucial to Jung during his presidency of the General

Medical Society for Psychotherapy (renamed the International General Medical Society for Psychotherapy [IGMSP]) as a condition of Jung's acceptance of the role in 1933 (Vannoy Adams and Sherry, 1991/2003: 226–27). As vice-president of the same organisation in 1938, Crichton-Miller supported Jung's general goal of promoting the non-German membership of the society to counteract the increasing German influence. By 1939, there was growing pressure from Professor Matthias Göring (head of the German General Medical Society for Psychotherapy from 1936 to 1945 and elder cousin of the Reichsmarschall, Herman Göring) to admit Italy, Hungary and Japan, a move that would have strengthened the influence of the Axis countries in the society (Adler [ed.], 1973: 286 n.1). In what he describes as a 'decisive showdown with the Germans in Zurich' (Jung, 1961/1989b: 640), Jung knew that Crichton-Miller's support as vice-president, and as a 'representative of higher reason', would be pivotal (Adler [ed.], 1973: 271). In a letter to Crichton-Miller dated 28 June 1939, Jung admits that the suspicion surrounding his alleged collaboration with the Nazis made Crichton-Miller's presence all the more important (ibid.: 271–72). The founder of the Tavistock did not disappoint. Jung recounts that, as vice-president of the IGMSP, Crichton-Miller 'lent him personally his invaluable help to ward off the German intrigue' (Jung, 1961/1989b: 640), which incurred the indignation of Professor Göring (Adler [ed.], 1973: 275 n.1). Jung was 'forever grateful' for Crichton-Miller's 'sturdy co-operation' and 'loyal friendship' (Jung, 1961/1989b: 640).

Alongside Crichton-Miller, Hadfield also played a role in cultivating the early eclectic and integrative atmosphere of the Tavistock. In particular, Hadfield was influential in shaping the psychotherapeutic training offered by the clinic. Like Crichton-Miller, Hadfield was interested in the relation between mind and brain. He had practised hypnosis on shell-shock victims in WWI and was responsible for 'the "training analysis" of many younger psychiatrists in the 1930s' (Hinshelwood, 2013: 46). He wrote extensively and was psychoanalytic in his thinking, though his efforts were nonetheless 'regularly panned by Ernest Jones on the grounds of being divergent from Freudian psychoanalysis' (ibid.). Hadfield's divergence from classical psychoanalytic thinking was probably informed by his preference for Jung, cultivated, no doubt, during his time at Oxford, where he learned from William McDougall (ibid.).

McDougall, an English psychologist and co-founder of the British Psychological Society, is probably best known for his An Introduction to Social Psychology (1908/1998). Like many psychologists of his time, McDougall treated shell-shock victims during WWI. The start of the war in 1914 also interrupted his analysis with C. G. Jung. The potential influence Jung had on McDougall is more evident in his later life, when his research interests 'veered towards psychic phenomena and Lamarckian inheritance', and served to alienate him from his colleagues (Richards, 2004: 331). McDougall also claimed to have anticipated certain psychoanalytic ideas that were becoming more mainstream and accepted. He is ultimately remembered for 'the range of perspectives he sought to integrate' and his insistence on maintaining 'a teleological approach to understanding human nature' (ibid.: 332). Such a focus finds no better expression than in Jung's psychology. It is not surprising, then, that Hadfield – as McDougall's student – developed a distinctly Jungian orientation. Nor is it surprising that Hadfield, as one of the original figures appointed by Crichton-Miller in 1920 and named Director of Studies in 1933, extended an invitation to Jung to deliver a set of lectures to the Institute of Medical Psychology, between September 30th and October 4th, 1935. When Jung wished to build stronger links between the IGMSP and an 'Anglo-Saxon organization', he did not hesitate to contact Hadfield for his opinion (Adler [ed.], 1973: 202–03). What I am suggesting, and what I have tried to show, is that the lectures themselves were given at a crucial point in Jung's life. They provide a particularly advantageous vertex from which we may critically assess the development of analytical psychology – as a clinical approach, depth psychological theory and academic discipline.

In addition to providing an invaluable starting point for the contextualization of Jung's thinking in relation to that of his contemporaries, as well as affording an answer to the question, 'Why was Jung invited to the Tavistock Clinic in 1935?', the lectures are relevant because they serve as an excellent introduction to analytical psychology. Not only are the major tenets of Jung's thinking covered throughout, but his mindfulness of his audience – some of whom, as we have noted, were situated on the periphery of depth psychology and included medical professionals, journalists and writers – certainly informed the way in which he presented his theories. Jung's style of presentation, combined with the discussions that prompted clarification from Jung (albeit at times defensive in tone and rhetorical in style), make for a lively read. Of particular value are the numerous clinical vignettes that Jung intersperses. Unlike Freud, Jung is not known for writing detailed case studies demonstrating how he applied theory to, and how he distilled theory from, the practice of analysis and dream interpretation. However problematic Freud's case studies may be (Borch-Jacobsen and Shamdasani, 2012: 179–234), they are rich resources for those interested in psychoanalytic thinking and technique. While Jung's 'Tavistock Lectures' cannot and should not, in all fairness, be considered an equivalent to Freud's case histories, they do clearly communicate, and conveniently locate in one volume, Jung's approach to dreams. More importantly, Jung's inclusion of clinical vignettes throughout the lectures reminds us that Jung's theory-building was not only the result of a 'subjective confession' (Jung, 1931/1961: 336), but one steeped in 'empirical' research, a point he staunchly defended numerous times during his lifetime (see Jung, 1952/1989: 663). For all of these reasons, I am delighted that *Analytical Psychology: Its Theory and Practice* is now a part of the Routledge Classics series, so that it may be enjoyed and appreciated on multiple levels. The text provides a rare snapshot of Jung's charisma and 'rudeness', and captures both the complexity and simplicity of his thinking. Most importantly, while I have no doubt that the text will be critically assessed by many, I hope that it will be cherished for its beauty by all.

NOTES

1   Also present was Eric Benjamin Strauss, who was a member of the Organizing Committee of the congress held at Oxford in 1938 (Adler [ed.], 1973: 242). Strauss – an assistant physician at the Institute of Medical Psychology at the time – participated in discussions one, two and four of Jung's 'Tavistock Lectures'.
2   As indicated in E. A. Bennet's original Foreword, the Tavistock Square Clinic (also known as the Tavistock Clinic for Functional Nerve Cases [Adler {ed.}, 1973: 271]) was founded in 1920. The name was changed to The Institute of Medical Psychology in 1931 and again a few years later to The Tavistock Clinic (Bennet, 1968: xiii, n.1).
3   The main correspondence is housed in the Bollingen Archive at the Library of Congress. A thorough investigation of Fordham's papers held in the Wellcome Archives might also prove fruitful (Shamdasani, personal communication).

REFERENCES

Adler, Gerhard (ed.). (1973). *C. G. Jung Letters, Volume 1: 1906–1950*. London: Routledge & Kegan Paul.

Bair, Deirdre. (2003). *Jung: A Biography*. New York and Boston: Little, Brown and Company.

Bennet, E. A. (1968). 'Foreword' in C. G. Jung, *Analytical Psychology: Its Theory and Practice: (The Tavistock Lectures)*. London: Routledge & Kegan Paul, pp. xiii–xvi.

Borch-Jacobsen, Mikkel and Shamdasani, Sonu. (2012). *The Freud Files: An Inquiry into the History of Psychoanalysis*. Cambridge: Cambridge University Press.

Campbell, Julie. (2005). 'The Entrapment of the Female Body in Beckett's Plays in Relation to Jung's Third Tavistock Lecture' in *Samuel Beckett Today/Aujourd'hui*, 15, pp. 161–72.

Hayman, Ronald. (1999/2002). *A Life of Jung*. London: Bloomsbury.

Hinshelwood, Robert D. (2013). 'The Tavistock Years' in Robert D. Hinshelwood and Nuno Torres (eds), *Bion's Sources: The Shaping of his Paradigms*. Hove: Routledge, pp. 44–55.

Jung, C. G. (1931/1961). 'Freud and Jung: Contrasts' in Sir Herbert Read, Michael Fordham, Gerhard Adler and William McGuire (eds), *The Collected Works of C. G. Jung, Volume 4: Freud and Psychoanalysis*. R. F. C. Hull (trans.). London: Routledge & Kegan Paul, pp. 333–40.

———. (1936). *Fundamental Psychological Conceptions: A Report of Five Lectures by C. G. Jung.* Mary Barker and Margaret Game (eds) for the Analytical Psychology Club, London.

———. (1952/1989). 'A Reply to Martin Buber' in Sir Herbert Read, Michael Fordham, Gerhard Adler and William McGuire (eds), *The Collected Works of C. G. Jung, Volume 18: The Symbolic Life, Miscellaneous Writings.* R. F. C. Hull (trans.). Princeton, NJ: Princeton University Press, pp. 663–70.

———. (1961/1989a). *Memories, Dreams, Reflections.* Recorded and edited by Aniela Jaffé. Richard and Clara Winston (trans.). New York: Vintage Books.

———. (1961/1989b). 'Foreword to "Hugh Crichton-Miller, 1877–1959" ' in Sir Herbert Read, Michael Fordham, Gerhard Adler and William McGuire (eds), *The Collected Works of C. G. Jung, Volume 18: The Symbolic Life, Miscellaneous Writings.* R. F. C. Hull (trans.). Princeton, NJ: Princeton University Press, pp. 639–41.

———. (1968). *Analytical Psychology: Its Theory and Practice.* London: Routledge & Kegan Paul Ltd.

McDougall, William. (1908/1998). *An Introduction to Social Psychology.* Bristol: Thoemmes.

McGuire, William (ed.). (1974). *The Freud/Jung Letters: the Correspondence between Sigmund Freud and C. G. Jung.* Ralph Manheim and R. F. C. Hull (trans.). Princeton, NJ: Princeton University Press.

Richards, Graham. (2004). 'McDougall, William (1871–1938)' in H. C. G. Matthew and Brian Harrison (eds), *Oxford Dictionary of National Biography, Volume 35, Macan–Macpherson.* Oxford: Oxford University Press.

Samuels, Andrew. (1988). 'Foreword' in C. G. Jung, *Essays on Contemporary Events: Reflections on Nazi Germany.* London: Ark Paperbacks.

Shamdasani, Sonu. (2005–2006). 'From the Uncollected Jung: Jung in Oxford, 1938' in *Jung History: A Semi-Annual Publication of the Philemon Foundation,* 1(2), pp. 3–5.

Torres, Nuno and Hinshelwood, Robert D. (2013). 'The Wider Medical Culture of Bion's Bio-psycho-social Framework' in Robert D. Hinshelwood and Nuno Torres (eds), *Bion's Sources: The Shaping of his Paradigms.* London: Routledge, pp. 35–43.

Vannoy Adams, Michael and Sherry, Jay. (1991/2003). 'Appendix A. Significant Words and Events. Revised and Updated by Jay Sherry' in Aryeh Maidenbaum (ed.), *Jung and the Shadow of Anti-Semitism.* Berwick, ME: Nicolas-Hays, Inc., pp. 219–57.

THE TAVISTOCK LECTURES

LECTURE ONE

The Chairman (Dr H. Crichton-Miller):

Ladies and Gentlemen, I am here to express your welcome to Professor Jung, and it gives me great pleasure to do so. We have looked forward, Professor Jung, to your coming for several months with happy anticipation. Many of us no doubt have looked forward to these seminars hoping for new light. Most of us, I trust, are looking forward to them hoping for new light upon ourselves. Many have come here because they look upon you as the man who has saved modern psychology from a dangerous isolation in the range of human knowledge and science into which it was drifting. Some of us have come here because we respect and admire that breadth of vision with which you have boldly made the alliance between philosophy and psychology which has been so condemned in certain other quarters. You have restored for us the idea of value, the concept of human freedom in psychological thought; you have given us certain new ideas that to many of us have been very precious, and above all things you have not relinquished the study of the human psyche at the point where all science ends. For this and many other benefits which are known to each of us independently and individually we are grateful to you, and we anticipate with the highest expectations these meetings.

Professor Jung:

Ladies and Gentlemen: First of all I should like to point out that my mother tongue is not English; thus if my English is not too good I must ask your forgiveness for any error I may commit.

As you know, my purpose is to give you a short outline of certain fundamental conceptions of psychology. If my demonstration is chiefly concerned with my own principles or my own point of view, it is not that I overlook the value of the great contributions of other workers in this field. I do not want to push myself unduly into the foreground, but I can surely expect my audience to be as much aware of Freud's and Adler's merits as I am.

Now as to our procedure, I should like to give you first a short idea of my programme. We have two main topics to deal with, namely, on the one side the concepts concerning the *structure of the unconscious mind* and its *contents*; on the other, the *methods* used in the *investigation* of contents originating in the unconscious psychic processes. The second topic falls into three parts, first, the word-association method; second, the method of dream-analysis; and third, the method of active imagination.

I know, of course, that I am unable to give you a full account of all there is to say about such difficult topics as, for instance, the philosophical, religious, ethical, and social problems peculiar to the collective consciousness of our time, or the processes of the collective unconscious and the comparative mythological and historical researches necessary for their elucidation. These topics, although apparently remote, are yet the most potent factors in making, regulating, and disturbing the personal mental condition, and they also form the root of disagreement in the field of psychological theories. Although I am a medical man and therefore chiefly concerned with psychopathology, I am nevertheless convinced that this particular branch of psychology can only be benefited by a considerably deepened and more extensive knowledge of the normal psyche in general. The doctor especially should never lose sight of the fact that diseases are disturbed normal processes and not *entia per se* with a psychology exclusively their own. *Similia similibus curantur* is a remarkable truth of the old medicine, and as a great truth it is also liable to become great nonsense. Medical psychology, therefore, should be careful not to become morbid itself. One-sidedness and restriction of horizon are well-known neurotic peculiarities.

Whatever I may be able to tell you will undoubtedly remain a regrettably unfinished torso. Unfortunately I take little stock of new theories, as my empirical temperament is more eager for new facts than for what one might speculate about them, although this is, I must admit, an enjoyable intellectual pastime. Each new case is almost a new theory to me, and I am not quite convinced that this standpoint is a thoroughly bad one, particularly when one considers the extreme youth of modern psychology, which to my mind has not yet left its cradle. I know, therefore, that the time for general theories is not yet ripe. It even looks to me sometimes as if psychology had not yet understood either the gigantic size of its task, or the perplexingly and distressingly complicated nature of its subject-matter: the psyche itself. It seems as if we were just waking up to this fact, and that the dawn is still too dim for us to realize in full what it means that the psyche, being the *object* of scientific observation and judgment, is at the same time its *subject*, the *means* by which you make such observations. The menace of so formidably vicious a circle has driven me to an extreme of caution and relativism which has often been thoroughly misunderstood.

I do not want to disturb our dealings by bringing up disquieting critical arguments. I only mention them as a sort of anticipatory excuse for seemingly unnecessary complications. I am not troubled by theories, but a great deal by facts; and I beg you therefore to keep in mind that the shortness of time at my disposal does not allow me to produce all the circumstantial evidence which would substantiate my conclusions. I especially refer here to the intricacies of dream-analysis and to the comparative method of investigating the unconscious processes. In short, I have to depend a great deal upon your goodwill, but I realize naturally it is my own task in the first place to make things as plain as possible.

Psychology is a science of consciousness, in the very first place. In the second place, it is the science of the products of what we call the unconscious psyche. We cannot directly explore the unconscious psyche because the unconscious is just unconscious, and we have therefore no relation to it. We can only deal with the conscious products which we suppose have originated in the field called the unconscious, that field of 'dim representations' which the philosopher Kant in his *Anthropology*[1] speaks of as being half a world. Whatever we have to say about the unconscious is what the conscious mind says about it. Always the unconscious psyche, which is entirely of an unknown nature, is expressed by consciousness and in terms of consciousness, and that is the only thing we can do. We cannot go beyond that, and we should always keep it in mind as an ultimate critique of our judgment.

Consciousness is a peculiar thing. It is an intermittent phenomenon. One-fifth, or one-third, or perhaps even one-half of our human life is spent in an unconscious condition. Our early childhood is unconscious. Every night we sink into the unconscious, and only in phases between waking and sleeping have we a more or less clear consciousness. To a certain extent it is even questionable how clear that consciousness is. For instance, we assume that a boy or girl ten years of age would be conscious, but one could easily prove that it is a very peculiar kind of consciousness, for it might be a consciousness without any consciousness of the *ego*. I know a number of cases of children eleven, twelve, and fourteen years of age, or even older, suddenly realizing 'I am'. For the first time in their lives they know that they themselves are experiencing, that they are looking back over a past in which they can remember things happening but cannot remember that they were in them.

We must admit that when we say 'I' we have no absolute criterion whether we have a full experience of 'I' or not. It might be that our realization of the ego is still fragmentary and that in some future time people will know very much more about what the ego means to man than we do. As a matter of fact, we cannot see where that process might ultimately end.

Consciousness is like a surface or a skin upon a vast unconscious area of unknown extent. We do not know how far the unconscious rules because we simply know nothing of it. You cannot say anything about a thing of which you know nothing. When we say 'the unconscious' we often mean to convey something by the term, but as a matter of fact we simply convey that we do not know what the unconscious is. We have only indirect proofs that there is a mental sphere which is subliminal. We have some scientific justification for our conclusion that it exists. From the products which that unconscious mind produces we can draw certain conclusions as to its possible nature. But we must be careful not to be too anthropomorphic in our conclusions, because things might in reality be very different from what our consciousness makes them.

If, for instance, you look at our physical world and if you compare what our consciousness makes of this same world, you find all sorts of mental pictures which do not exist as objective facts. For instance, we see colour and hear sound, but in reality they are oscillations. As a matter of fact, we need a laboratory with very complicated apparatus in order to establish a picture of that world apart from our senses and apart from our psyche; and I suppose it is very much the same with our unconscious – we ought to have a laboratory in which we could establish by objective methods how things really are when in an unconscious condition. So any conclusion or any statement I make in the course of my lectures about the unconscious should be taken with that critique in mind. It is always *as if*, and you should never forget that restriction.

The conscious mind moreover is characterized by a certain narrowness. It can hold only a few simultaneous contents at a given moment. All the rest is unconscious at the time, and we only get a sort of continuation or a general understanding or awareness of a conscious world through the *succession* of conscious moments. We can never hold an image of totality because our consciousness is too narrow; we can only see flashes of existence. It is always as if we were observing through a slit so that we only see a particular moment; all the rest is dark and we are not aware of it at that moment. The area of the unconscious is enormous and always continuous, while the area of consciousness is a restricted field of momentary vision.

Consciousness is very much the product of perception and orientation in the *external* world. It is probably localized in the *cerebrum*, which is of ectodermic origin and was probably a sense organ of the skin at the time of our remote ancestors. The consciousness derived from that localization in the brain therefore probably retains these qualities of sensation and orientation. Peculiarly enough, the French and English psychologists of the early seventeenth and eighteenth centuries tried to derive consciousness from the senses as if it consisted solely of sense data. That is expressed by the famous formula *Nihil est in intellectu quod non fuerit in sensu*.[2] You can observe something similar in modern psychological theories. Freud, for instance, does not derive the conscious from sense data, but he derives the unconscious from the conscious, which is along the same rational line.

I would put it the reverse way: I would say the thing that comes first is obviously the unconscious and that consciousness really arises from an unconscious condition. In early childhood we are unconscious; the most important functions of an instinctive nature are unconscious, and consciousness is rather the product of the unconscious. It is a condition which demands a violent effort. You get tired from being conscious. You get exhausted by consciousness. It is an almost unnatural effort. When you observe primitives, for instance, you will see that on the slightest provocation or with no provocation whatever they doze off, they disappear. They sit for hours on end, and when you ask them, 'What are you doing? What are you thinking?' they are offended, because they say, 'Only a man that is crazy thinks – he has thoughts in his head. We do not think'. If they think at all, it is rather in the belly or in the heart. Certain Negro tribes assure you that thoughts are in the belly because they only realize those thoughts which actually disturb the liver, intestines, or stomach. In other words, they are conscious only of emotional thoughts. Emotions and affects are always accompanied by obvious physiological innervations.

The Pueblo Indians told me that all Americans are crazy, and of course I was somewhat astonished and asked them why. They said, 'Well, they say they think in their heads. No sound man thinks in the head. *We* think in the heart'. They are just about in the Homeric age, when the diaphragm (*phren* = mind, soul) was the seat of psychic activity. That means a psychic localization of a different nature. Our concept of consciousness supposes thought to be in our most dignified head. But the Pueblo Indians derive consciousness from the intensity of feeling. Abstract thought does not exist for them. As the Pueblo Indians are sun-worshippers, I tried the argument of St Augustine on them. I told them that God is not the sun but the one who made the sun.[3] They could not accept this because they cannot go beyond the perceptions of their senses and their feelings. Therefore consciousness and thought to them are localized in the heart. To us, on the other hand, psychic activities are nothing. We hold that dreams and fantasies are localized 'down below', therefore there are people who speak of the sub-conscious mind, of the things that are *below* consciousness.

These peculiar localizations play a great role in so-called primitive psychology, which is by no means primitive. For instance if you study Tantric

Yoga and Hindu psychology you will find the most elaborate system of psychic layers, of localizations of consciousness up from the region of the perineum to the top of the head. These 'centres' are the so-called *chakras*.[4] and you not only find them in the teachings of yoga but can discover the same idea in old German alchemical books,[5] which surely do not derive from a knowledge of yoga.

The important fact about consciousness is that nothing can be conscious without an ego to which it refers. If something is not related to the ego then it is not conscious. Therefore you can define consciousness as a relation of psychic facts to the ego. What is that ego? The ego is a complex datum which is constituted first of all by a general awareness of your body, of your existence, and secondly by your memory data; you have a certain idea of having been, a long series of memories. Those two are the main constituents of what we call the ego. Therefore you can call the ego a complex of psychic facts. This complex has a great power of attraction, like a magnet; it attracts contents from the unconscious, from that dark realm of which we know nothing; it also attracts impressions from the outside, and when they enter into association with the ego they are conscious. If they do not, they are not conscious.

My idea of the ego is that it is a sort of complex. Of course, the nearest and dearest complex which we cherish is our ego. It is always in the centre of our attention and of our desires, and it is the absolutely indispensable centre of consciousness. If the ego becomes split up, as in schizophrenia, all sense of values is gone, and also things become inaccessible for voluntary reproduction because the centre has split and certain parts of the psyche refer to one fragment of the ego and certain other contents to another fragment of the ego. Therefore, with a schizophrenic, you often see a rapid change from one personality into another.

You can distinguish a number of functions in consciousness. They enable consciousness to become oriented in the field of ectopsychic facts and endopsychic facts. What I understand by the *ectopsyche* is a system of relationship between the contents of consciousness and facts and data coming in from the environment. It is a system of orientation which concerns my dealing with the external facts given to me by the function of my senses. The *endopsyche*, on the other hand, is a system of relationship between the contents of consciousness and postulated processes in the unconscious.

In the first place we will speak of the ectopsychic functions. First of all we have *sensation*,[6] our sense function. By sensation I understand what the French psychologists call 'la fonction du réel', which is the sum-total of my awareness of external facts given to me through the function of my senses. So I think that the French term 'la fonction du réel' explains it in the most comprehensive way. Sensation tells me that something is: it does not tell me *what* it is and it does not tell me other things about that something; it only tells me that something is.

The next function that is distinguishable is thinking.[7] Thinking, if you ask a philosopher, is something very difficult, so never ask a philosopher about it because he is the only man who does not know what thinking is. Everybody else knows what thinking is. When you say to a man, 'Now think properly', he knows exactly what you mean, but a philosopher never knows. Thinking in its simplest form tells you *what* a thing is. It gives a name to the thing. It adds a concept because thinking is perception and judgment. (German psychology calls it apperception.)[8]

The third function you can distinguish and for which ordinary language has a term is feeling.[9] Here minds become very confused and people get angry when I speak about feeling, because according to their view I say something very dreadful about it. Feeling informs you through its feeling-tones of the *values* of things. Feeling tells you for instance whether a thing is acceptable or agreeable or not. It tells you what a thing is *worth* to you. On account of that phenomenon, you cannot perceive and you cannot apperceive without having a certain feeling reaction. You always have a certain feeling-tone, which you can even demonstrate by experiment. We will talk of these things later on. Now the 'dreadful' thing about feeling is that it is, like thinking, a *rational*[10] function. All men who think are absolutely convinced that feeling is never a rational function but, on the contrary, most irrational. Now I say: Just be patient for a while and realize that man cannot be perfect in every respect. If a man is perfect in his thinking he is surely never perfect in his feeling, because you cannot do the two things at the same time; they hinder each other. Therefore when you want to think in a dispassionate way, really scientifically or philosophically, you must get away from all feeling-values. You cannot be bothered with feeling-values at the same time, otherwise you begin to feel that it is far more important to think about the freedom of the will than, for instance, about the classification of lice. And certainly if you approach from the point of view of feeling the two objects are not only different as to *facts* but also as to *value*. Values are no anchors for the intellect, but they exist and giving value is an important psychological function. If you want to have a complete picture of the world you must necessarily consider values. If you do not, you will get into trouble. To many people feeling appears to be most irrational, because you feel all sorts of things in foolish moods: therefore everybody is convinced, in this country particularly, that you should control your feelings. I quite admit that this is a good habit and wholly admire the English for that faculty. Yet there are such things as feelings, and I have seen people who control their feelings marvellously well and yet are terribly bothered by them.

Now the fourth function. Sensation tells us that a thing *is*. Thinking tells us *what* that thing is, feeling tells us what it is *worth* to us. Now what else could there be? One would assume one has a complete picture of the world when one knows there *is* something, *what* it is, and what it is *worth*. But there is another category, and that is time. Things have a past and they have a future. They come from somewhere, they go to somewhere, and you cannot see where they came from and you cannot know where they go to, but you get what the Americans call a hunch. For instance, if you are a dealer in art or in old furniture you get a hunch that a certain object is by a very good master of 1720, you get a hunch that it is good work. Or you do not know what shares will do after a while, but you get the hunch that they will rise. That is what is called intuition,[11] a sort of divination, a sort of miraculous faculty. For instance, you do not know that your patient has something on his mind of a very painful kind, but you 'get an idea', you 'have a certain feeling', as we say, because ordinary language is not yet developed enough for one to have suitably defined terms. But the word intuition becomes more and more a part of the English language, and you are very fortunate because in other languages that word does not exist. The Germans cannot even make a linguistic distinction between sensation and feeling. It is different in French; if you speak French you cannot possibly say that you have a certain 'sentiment dans l'estomac', you will say 'sensation'; in English you also have your distinctive words for sensation and feeling. But you can mix up *feeling* and *intuition* easily. Therefore it is an almost artificial distinction I make here, though for practical reasons it is most important that we make such a differentiation in scientific language. We must define what we mean when we use certain terms, otherwise we talk an unintelligible language, and in psychology this is always a misfortune. In ordinary conversation, when a man says feeling, he means possibly something entirely different from another fellow who also talks about feeling. There are any number of psychologists who use the word *feeling*, and they define it as a sort of crippled thought. 'Feeling is nothing but an unfinished thought' – that is the definition of a well-known psychologist. But feeling is something genuine, it is something real, it is a function, and therefore we have a word for it. The instinctive natural mind always finds the words that designate things which really have existence. Only psychologists invent words for things that do not exist.

The last-defined function, intuition, seems to be very mysterious, and you know I am 'very mystical,' as people say. This then is one of my pieces of mysticism! Intuition is a function by which you see round corners, which you really cannot do; yet the fellow will do it for you and you trust him. It is a function which normally you do not use if you live a regular life within four walls and do regular routine work. But if you are on the Stock Exchange or in Central Africa, you will use your hunches like anything. You cannot, for instance, calculate whether when you turn round a corner in the bush you will meet a rhinoceros or a tiger – but you get a hunch, and it will perhaps save your life. So you see that people who live exposed to natural conditions use intuition a great deal, and people who risk something in an unknown field, who are pioneers of some sort, will use intuition. Inventors will use it and judges will use it. Whenever you have to deal with strange conditions where you have no established values or established concepts, you will depend upon that faculty of intuition.

I have tried to describe that function as well as I can, but perhaps it is not very good. I say that intuition is a sort of perception which does not go exactly by the senses, but it goes via the unconscious, and at that I leave it and say 'I don't know how it works'. I do not know what is happening when a man knows something he definitely should not know. I do not know how he has come by it, but he has it all right and he can act on it. For instance, anticipatory dreams, telepathic phenomena, and all that kind of thing are intuitions. I have seen plenty of them, and I am convinced that they do exist. You can see these things also with primitives. You can see them everywhere if you pay attention to these perceptions that somehow work through the subliminal data, such as sense-perceptions so feeble that our consciousness simply cannot take them in. Sometimes, for instance, in cryptomnesia, some-thing creeps up into consciousness; you catch a word which gives you a suggestion, but it is always something that is unconscious until the moment it appears, and so presents itself as if it had fallen from heaven. The Germans call this an Einfall, which means a thing which falls into your head from nowhere. Sometimes it is like a revelation. Actually, intuition is a very natural function, a perfectly normal thing, and it is necessary, too, because it makes up for what you cannot perceive or think or feel because it lacks reality. You see, the past is not real any more and the future is not as real as we think. Therefore we must be very grateful to heaven that we have such a function which gives us a certain light on those things which are round the corners. Doctors, of course, being often presented with the most unheard-of situa-tions, need intuition a great deal. Many a good diagnosis comes from this 'very mysterious' function.

Psychological functions are usually controlled by the will, or we hope they are, because we are afraid of everything that moves by itself. When the func-tions are controlled they can be excluded from use, they can be suppressed, they can be selected, they can be increased in intensity, they can be directed by willpower, by what we call intention. But they also can function in an involuntary way, that is, they think for you, they feel for you – very often they do this and you cannot even stop them. Or they function unconsciously so that you do not know what they have done, though you might be presented, for instance, with the result of a feeling process which has happened in the unconscious. Afterwards somebody will probably say, 'Oh, you were very angry, or you were offended, and therefore you reacted in such and such a way'. Perhaps you are quite unconscious that you have felt in that way, nevertheless it is most probable that you have. Psychological functions, like the sense functions, have their specific energy. You cannot dispose of feeling, or of thinking, or of any of the four functions. No one can say, 'I will not think' – he will think inevitably. People cannot say, 'I will not feel' – they will feel because the specific energy invested in each function expresses itself and cannot be exchanged for another.

Of course, one has preferences. People who have a good mind prefer to think about things and to adapt by thinking. Other people who have a good feeling function are good social mixers, they have a great sense of values; they are real artists in creating feeling situations and living by feeling situations. Or a man with a keen sense of objective observation will use his sensation chiefly, and so on. The dominating function gives each individual his particular kind of psychology. For example, when a man uses chiefly his intellect, he will be of an unmistakable type, and you can deduce from that fact the condition of his feeling. When thinking is the dominant or superior function, feeling is necessarily in an inferior condition.[12] The same rule applies to the other three functions. But I will show you that with a diagram which will make it clear.

You can make the so-called cross of the functions (Figure 1). In the centre is the ego (E), which has a certain amount of energy at its disposal, and that energy is the will-power. In the case of the thinking type, that will-power can be directed to thinking (T). Then we must put feeling (F) down below, because it is, in this case, the inferior function.[13] That comes from the fact that when you think you must exclude feeling, just as when you feel you must exclude thinking. If you are thinking, leave feeling and feeling-values alone, because

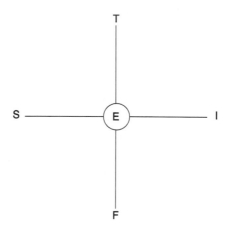

Figure 1 The Functions

feeling is most upsetting to your thoughts. On the other hand people who go by feeling-values leave thinking well alone, and they are right to do so, because these two different functions contradict each other. People have sometimes assured me that their thinking was just as differentiated as their feeling, but I could not believe it, because an individual cannot have the two opposites in the same degree of perfection at the same time.

The same is the case with *sensation* (S) and intuition (I). How do they affect each other? When you are observing physical facts you cannot see round corners at the same time. When you observe a man who is working by his sense function you will see, if you look at him attentively, that the axes of his eyes have a tendency to converge and to come together at one point. When you study the expression or the eyes of intuitive people, you will see that they only glance at things – they do not look, they radiate at things because they take in their fullness, and among the many things they perceive they get one point on the periphery of their field of vision and that is the hunch. Often you can tell from the eyes whether people are intuitive or not. When you have an intuitive attitude you usually do not observe the details. You try always to take in the whole of a situation, and then suddenly something crops up out of this wholeness. When you are a sensation type you will observe facts as they are, but then you have no intuition, simply because the two things cannot be done at the same time. It is too difficult, because the principle of the one function excludes the principle of the other function. That is why I put them here as opposites.

Now, from this simple diagram you can arrive at quite a lot of very important conclusions as to the structure of a given consciousness. For instance, if you find that thinking is highly differentiated, then feeling is undifferentiated. What does that mean? Does it mean these people have no feelings? No, on the contrary. They say, 'I have very strong feelings. I am full of emotion and temperament'. These people are under the sway of their emotions, they are caught by their emotions, they are overcome by their emotions at times. If, for instance, you study the private life of professors it is a very interesting study. If you want to be fully informed as to how the intellectual behaves at home, ask his wife and she will be able to tell you a story!

The reverse is true of the *feeling* type. The feeling type, if he is natural, never allows himself to be disturbed by thinking; but when he gets sophisticated and somewhat neurotic he is disturbed by thoughts. Then thinking appears in a compulsory way, he cannot get away from certain thoughts. He is a very nice chap, but he has extraordinary convictions and ideas, and his thinking is of an inferior kind. He is caught by this thinking, entangled in certain thoughts; he cannot disentangle because he cannot reason, his thoughts are not movable. On the other hand, an intellectual, when caught by his feelings, says, 'I feel just like that', and there is no argument against it. Only when he is thoroughly boiled in his emotion will he come out of it again. He cannot be reasoned out of his feeling, and he would be a very incomplete man if he could.

The same happens with the *sensation* type and the *intuitive* type. The intuitive is always bothered by the reality of things; he fails from the standpoint of realities; he is always out for the possibilities of life. He is the man who plants a field and before the crop is ripe is off again to a new field. He has ploughed fields behind him and new hopes ahead all the time, and nothing comes off. But the sensation type remains with things. He remains in a given reality. To him a thing is true when it is real. Consider what it means to an intuitive when something is real. It is just the wrong thing; it should not be, something else should be. But when a sensation type does not have a given reality – four walls in which to be – he is sick. Give the intuitive type four walls in which to be, and the only thing is how to get out of it, because to him a given situation is a prison which must be undone in the shortest time so that he can be off to new possibilities.

These differences play a very great role in practical psychology. Do not think I am putting people into this box or that and saying, 'He is an intuitive', or 'He is a thinking type'. People often ask me, 'Now, is So-and-So not a thinking type?' I say, 'I never thought about it', and I did not. It is no use at all putting people into drawers with different labels. But when you have a large empirical material, you need critical principles of order to help you to classify it. I hope I do not exaggerate, but to me it is very important to be able to create a kind of order in my empirical material, particularly when people are troubled and confused or when you have to explain them to somebody else. For instance, if you have to explain a wife to a husband or a husband to a wife, it is often very helpful to have these objective criteria, otherwise the whole thing remains 'He said' – 'She said'.

As a rule, the inferior function does not possess the qualities of a conscious differentiated function. The conscious differentiated function can as a rule be handled by intention and by the will. If you are a real thinker, you can direct your thinking by your will, you can control your thoughts. You are not the slave of your thoughts, you can think of something else. You can say, 'I can think something quite different, I can think the contrary'. But the feeling type can never do that because he cannot get rid of his thought. The thought possesses him, or rather he is possessed by thought. Thought has a fascination for him, therefore he is afraid of it. The intellectual type is afraid of being caught by feeling because his feeling has an archaic quality, and there he is like an archaic man – he is the helpless victim of his emotions. It is for this reason that primitive man is extraordinarily polite, he is very careful not to disturb the feelings of his fellows because it is dangerous to do so. Many of our customs are explained by that archaic politeness. For instance, it is not the custom to shake hands with somebody and keep your left hand in your pocket, or behind your back, because it must be visible that you do not carry a weapon in that hand. The Oriental greeting of bowing with hands extended palms upward means 'I have nothing in my hands'. If you kowtow you dip your head to the feet of the other man so that he sees you are absolutely defenceless and that you trust him completely. You can still study the symbolism of manners with primitives, and you can also see why they are afraid of the other fellow. In a similar way, we are afraid of our inferior functions. If you take a typical intellectual who is terribly afraid of falling in love, you will think his fear very foolish. But he is most probably right, because he will very likely make foolish nonsense when he falls in love. He will be caught most certainly, because his feeling only reacts to an archaic or to a dangerous type of woman. This is why many intellectuals are inclined to marry beneath them. They are caught by the landlady perhaps, or by the cook, because they are unaware of their archaic feeling through which they get caught. But they are right to be afraid, because their undoing will be in their feeling. Nobody can attack them in their intellect. There they are strong and can stand alone, but in their feelings they can be influenced, they can be caught, they can be cheated, and they know it. Therefore never force a man into his feeling when he is an intellectual. He controls it with an iron hand because it is very dangerous.

The same law applies to each function. The inferior function is always associated with an archaic personality in ourselves; in the inferior function we are all primitives. In our differentiated functions we are civilized and we are supposed to have free will; but there is no such thing as free will when it comes to the inferior function. There we have an open wound, or at least an open door through which anything might enter.

Now I am coming to the *endopsychic functions* of consciousness. The functions of which I have just spoken rule or help our conscious orientation in our relations with the environment; but they do not apply to the relation of things that are as it were below the ego. The ego is only a bit of consciousness which floats upon the ocean of the dark things. The dark things are the inner things. On that inner side there is a layer of psychic events that forms a sort of fringe of consciousness round the ego. I will illustrate it by a diagram (Figure 2).

If you suppose AA' to be the threshold of consciousness, then you would have in D an area of consciousness referring to the ectopsychic world B, the world ruled by those functions of which we were just speaking. But on the other side, in C, is the *shadow-world*. There the ego is somewhat dark, we do not see into it, we are an enigma to ourselves. We only know the ego in D, we do not know it in C. Therefore we are always discovering something new about ourselves. Almost every year something new turns up which we did not know before. We always think we are now at the end of our discoveries. We never

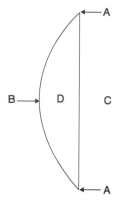

Figure 2 The Ego

are. We go on discovering that we are this, that, and other things, and some-times we have astounding experiences. That shows there is always a part of our personality which is still unconscious, which is still becoming; we are unfinished; we are growing and changing. Yet that future personality which we are to be in a year's time is already here, only it is still in the shadow. The ego is like a moving frame on a film. The future personality is not yet visible, but we are moving along, and presently we come to view the future being. These potentialities naturally belong to the dark side of the ego. We are well aware of what we have been, but we are not aware of what we are going to be.

Therefore the first function on that endopsychic side is memory. The function of memory, or reproduction, links us up with things that have faded out of consciousness, things that became subliminal or were cast away or repressed. What we call memory is this faculty to reproduce unconscious contents, and it is the first function we can clearly distinguish in its relationship between our consciousness and the contents that are actually not in view.

The *second* endopsychic function is a more difficult problem. We are now getting into deep waters because here we are coming into darkness. I will give you the name first: *the subjective components of conscious functions*. I hope I can make it clear. For instance, when you meet a man you have not seen before, naturally you think something about him. You do not always think things you would be ready to tell him immediately; perhaps you think things that are untrue, that do not really apply. Clearly, they are subjective reactions. The same reactions take place with things and with situations. Every application of a conscious function, whatever the object might be, is always accompanied by subjective reactions which are more or less inadmissible or unjust or inaccurate. You are painfully aware that these things happen in you, but nobody likes to admit that he is subject to such phenomena. He prefers to leave them in the shadow, because that helps him to assume that he is perfectly innocent and very nice and honest and straightforward and 'only too willing', etc. – you know all these phrases. As a matter of fact, one is not. One has any amount of subjective reactions, but it is not quite becoming to admit these things. These reactions I call the subjective components. They are a very important part of our relations to our own inner side. There things get definitely painful. That is why we dislike entering this shadow-world of the ego. We do not like to look at the shadow-side of ourselves; therefore there are many people in our civilized society who have lost their shadow altogether, they have got rid of it. They are only two-dimensional; they have lost the third dimension, and with it they have usually lost the body. The body is a most doubtful friend because it produces things we do not like; there are too many things about the body which cannot be mentioned. The body is very often the personification of this shadow of the ego. Sometimes it forms the skeleton in the cupboard, and everybody naturally wants to get rid of such a thing. I think this makes sufficiently clear what I mean by subjective components. They are usually a sort of disposition to react in a certain way, and usually the disposition is not altogether favourable.

There is one exception to this definition: a person who is not, as we suppose we all are, living on the positive side, putting the right foot forward and not the wrong one, etc. There are certain individuals whom we call in our Swiss dialect 'pitch-birds' [*Pechvögel*]; they are always getting into messes, they put their foot in it and always cause trouble, because they live their own shadow, they live their own negation. They are the sort of people who come late to a concert or a lecture, and because they are very modest and do not want to disturb other people, they sneak in at the end and then stumble over a chair and make a hideous racket so that everybody has to look at them. Those are the 'pitch-birds'.

Now we come to the third endopsychic component – I cannot say function. In the case of memory you can speak of a function, but even your memory is only to a certain extent a voluntary or controlled function. Very often it is exceedingly tricky; it is like a bad horse that cannot be mastered. It often refuses in the most embarrassing way. All the more is this the case with the subjective components and reactions. And now things begin to get worse, for this is where the *emotions* and *affects* come in. They are clearly not functions any more, they are just events, because in an emotion, as the word denotes, you are moved away, you are cast out, your decent ego is put aside, and something else takes your place. We say, 'He is beside himself', or 'The devil is riding him', or 'What has gotten into him today', because he is like a man who is possessed. The primitive does not say he got angry beyond measure; he says a spirit got into him and changed him completely. Something like that happens with emotions; you are simply possessed, you are no longer yourself, and your control is decreased practically to zero. That is a condition in which the inner side of a man takes hold of him, he cannot prevent it. He can clench his fists, he can keep quiet, but it has him nevertheless.

The fourth important endopsychic factor is what I call invasion. Here the shadow-side, the unconscious side, has full control so that it can break into the conscious condition. Then the conscious control is at its lowest. Those are the moments in a human life which you do not necessarily call pathological; they are pathological only in the old sense of the word when pathology meant the science of the passions. In that sense you can call them pathological, but it is really an extraordinary condition in which a man is seized upon by his unconscious and when anything may come out of him. One can lose one's mind in a more or less normal way. For instance, we cannot assume that the cases our ancestors knew very well are abnormal, because they are perfectly normal phenomena among primitives. They speak of the devil or an incubus or a spirit going into a man, or of his soul leaving him, one of his separate souls – they often have as many as six. When his soul leaves him, he is in an altered condition because he is suddenly deprived of himself; he suffers a loss of self. That is a thing you can often observe in neurotic patients. On certain days, or from time to time, they suddenly lose their energy, they lose themselves, and they come under a strange influence. These phenomena are not in themselves pathological; they belong to the ordinary phenomenology of man, but if they become habitual we rightly speak of a neurosis. These are the things that lead to neurosis; but they are also exceptional conditions among normal people. To have overwhelming emotions is not in itself pathological, it is merely undesirable. We need not invent such a word as pathological for an undesirable thing, because there are other undesirable things in the world which are not pathological, for instance, tax-collectors.

DISCUSSION

Dr J. A. Hadfield:

In what sense do you use the word 'emotion'? You used the word 'feeling' rather in the sense in which many people here use the word 'emotion'. Do you give the term 'emotion' a special significance or not?

Professor Jung:

I am glad you have put that question, because there are usually great mistakes and misunderstandings concerning the use of the word emotion. Naturally everybody is free to use words as he likes, but in scientific language you are bound to cling to certain distinctions so that everyone knows what you are talking about. You will remember I explained 'feeling' as a function of valuing, and I do not attach any particular significance to feeling. I hold that feeling is a rational function if it is differentiated. When it is not differentiated it just happens, and then it has all the archaic qualities which can be summed up by the word 'unreasonable'. But conscious feeling is a rational function of discriminating values.

If you study emotions you will invariably find that you apply the word 'emotional' when it concerns a condition that is characterized by physiological innervations. Therefore you can measure emotions to a certain extent, not their psychic part but the physiological part. You know the James-Lange theory of affect.[14] I take emotion as affect, it is the same as 'something affects you'. It does something to you – it interferes with you. Emotion is the thing that carries you away. You are thrown out of yourself; you are beside yourself as if an explosion had moved you out of yourself and put you beside yourself. There is a quite tangible physiological condition which can be observed at the same time. So the difference would be this: feeling has no physical or tangible physiological manifestations, while emotion is characterized by an altered physiological condition. You know that the James-Lange theory of affect says that you only get really emotional when you are aware of the physiological alteration of your general condition. You can observe this when you are in a situation where you would most probably be angry. You know you are going to be angry, and then you feel the blood rushing up into your head, and then you are really angry, but not before. Before, you only know you are going to be angry, but when the blood rushes up into your head you are caught by your own anger, immediately the body is affected, and because you realize that you are getting excited, you are twice as angry as you ought to be. Then you are in a real emotion. But when you have feeling you have control. You are on top of the situation, and you can say, 'I have a very nice feeling or a very bad feeling about it'. Everything is quiet and nothing happens. You can quietly inform somebody, 'I hate you', very nicely. But when you say it spitefully you have an emotion. To say it quietly will not cause an emotion, either in yourself or in the other person. Emotions are most contagious, they are the real carriers of mental contagion. For instance, if you are in a crowd that is in an emotional condition, you cannot help yourself, you are in it too, you are caught by that emotion. But the feelings of other people do not concern you in the least, and for this reason you will observe that the differentiated feeling type usually has a cooling effect upon you, while the emotional person heats you up because the fire is radiating out of him all the time. You see the flame of that emotion in his face. By sympathy your sympathetic system gets disturbed, and you will show very much the same signs after a while. That is not so with feelings. Do I make myself clear?

Dr Henry V. Dicks:

May I ask, in continuation of that question, what is the relation in your view between affects and feelings?

Professor Jung:

It is a question of degree. If you have a value which is overwhelmingly strong for you it will become an emotion at a certain point, namely, when it reaches such an intensity as to cause a physiological innervation. All our mental processes probably cause slight physiological disturbances which are so small that we have not the means to demonstrate them. But we have a pretty sensitive method by which to measure emotions, or the physiological part of them, and that is the psychogalvanic effect.[15] It is based on the fact that the electrical resistance of the skin decreases under the influence of emotion. It does not decrease under the influence of feeling.

I will give you an example. I made the following experiment with my former Professor at the Clinic. He functioned as my test partner, and I had him in the laboratory under the apparatus for measuring the psychogalvanic effect. I told him to imagine something which was intensely disagreeable to him but of which he knew I was not aware, something unknown to me yet known to him and exceedingly painful. So he did. He was well acquainted with such experiments and gifted with great power of concentration, so he concentrated on something, and there was almost no visible disturbance of the electrical resistance of the skin; the current did not increase at all. Then I thought I had a hunch. That very morning I had observed certain signs of something going on and I guessed it must be hellishly disagreeable to my chief. So I thought, 'I am going to try something'. I simply said to him, 'Was not that the case of So-and-So?' – mentioning the name. Instantly there was a deluge of emotion. That was the emotion; the former reaction was the feeling.

It is a curious fact that hysterical pain does not cause contraction of the pupils, it is not accompanied by physiological innervation, and yet it is an intense pain. But physical pain causes contraction of the pupils. You can have an intense feeling and no physiological alteration; but as soon as you have physiological alteration you are possessed, you are dissociated, thrown out of your own house, and the house is then free for the devils.

Dr Eric Graham Howe:

Could we equate emotion and feeling with conation and cognition respectively? Whereas feeling corresponds to cognition, emotion is conative.

Professor Jung:

Yes, one could say that in philosophical terminology. I have no objection.

Dr Howe:

May I have another shot? Your classification into four functions, namely those of sensation, thinking, feeling, and intuition, seems to me to correspond with the one-, two-, three- and four-dimensional classification. You yourself used the word 'three-dimensional' referring to the human body, and you also said that intuition differed from the other three in that it was the function which included Time. Perhaps, therefore, it corresponds to a fourth dimension? In that case, I suggest that 'sensation' corresponds with one-dimensional, 'perceptual cognition' with two-dimensional, 'conceptional cognition' (which would correspond perhaps with your 'feeling') with three-dimensional, and 'intuition' with four-dimensional on this system of classification.

Professor Jung:

You can put it like that. Since intuition sometimes seems to function as if there were no space, and sometimes as if there were no time, you might say that I add a sort of fourth dimension. But one should not go too far. The concept of the fourth dimension does not produce facts. Intuition is something like H. G. Wells's Time Machine. You remember the time machine, that peculiar motor, which when you sit on it moves off with you into time instead of into space. It consists of four columns, three of which are always visible, but the fourth is visible only indistinctly because it represents the time element. I am sorry but the awkward fact is that intuition is something like this fourth column. There is such a thing as unconscious perception, or perception by ways which are unconscious to us. We have the empirical material to prove the existence of this function. I am sorry that there are such things. My intellect would wish for a clear-cut universe with no dim corners, but there are these cobwebs in the cosmos. Nevertheless I do not think there is anything mystical about intuition. Can you explain beyond any possibility of doubt why, for instance, some birds travel enormous distances, or the doings of caterpillars, butterflies, ants, or termites? There you have to deal with quite a number of questions. Or take the fact of water having the greatest density at 4° Centigrade. Why such a thing? Why has energy a limitation to quantum? Well, it has, and that is awkward; it is not right that such things should be, but they are. It is exactly like the old question, 'Why has God made flies?' – He just has.

Dr Wilfred R. Bion:

In your experiment why did you ask the Professor to think of an experience which was painful to himself and unknown to you? Do you think there is any significance in the fact that he knew you knew of the unpleasant experience in the second experiment and that this had some bearing on the difference of emotional reaction which he showed in the two examples you gave?

Professor Jung:

Yes, absolutely. My idea was based on the fact that when I know that my partner does not know, it is far more agreeable to me; but when I know that he knows too, it is a very different thing and is very disagreeable. In any doctor's life there are cases which are more or less painful when a colleague knows about them, and I knew almost for a certainty that if I gave him a hint that I knew, he would jump like a mine, and he did. That was my reason.

Dr Eric B. Strauss:

Would Dr Jung make clearer what he means when he says that feeling is a rational function? Further, I do not quite understand what Dr Jung means by feeling. Most of us when we employ the term feeling understand polarities such as pleasure, pain, tension, and relaxation. Further, Dr Jung claims that the distinction between feelings and emotions is only one of degree. If the distinction is only one of degree, how is it that he puts them on different sides of the frontier, so to speak? Still further, Dr Jung claims that one of the criteria or the chief criterion would be that feelings are unaccompanied by physiological change, whereas emotions are accompanied by such changes. Experiments conducted by Professor Freudlicher[16] in Berlin have, I think, shown clearly that simple feelings, in the sense of pleasure, pain, tension, and relaxation, are as a matter of fact accompanied by physiological changes, such as changes in the blood pressure, which can now be recorded by very accurate apparatus.

Professor Jung:

It is true that feelings, if they have an emotional character, are accompanied by physiological effects; but there are definitely feelings which do not change the physiological condition. These feelings are very mental, they are not of an emotional nature. That is the distinction I make. Inasmuch as feeling is a function of values, you will readily understand that this is not a physiological condition. It can be something as abstract as abstract thinking. You would not expect abstract thinking to be a physiological condition. Abstract thinking is what the term denotes. Differentiated thinking is rational; and so feeling can be rational in spite of the fact that many people mix up the terminology.

We must have a word for the giving of values. We must designate that particular function, as apart from others, and feeling is an apt term. Of course, you can choose any other word you like, only you must say so. I have absolutely no objection if the majority of thinking people come to the conclusion that feeling is a very bad word for it. If you say, 'We prefer to use another term', then you must choose another term to designate the function of valuing, because the fact of values remains and we must have a name for it. Usually the sense of values is expressed by the term 'feeling'. But I do not cling to the term at all. I am absolutely liberal as to terms, only I give the definition of terms so that I can say what I mean when I use such and such a term. If anybody says that feeling is an emotion or that feeling is a thing that causes heightened blood pressure, I have no objection. I only say that I do not use the word in that sense. If people should agree that it ought to be forbidden to use the word feeling in such a way as I do, I have no objection. The Germans have the words Empfindung and Gefühl. When you read Goethe or Schiller you find that even the poets mix up the two functions. German psychologists have already recommended the suppression of the word Empfindung for feeling, and propose that one should use the word Gefühl (feeling) for values, while the word Empfindung should be used for sensation. No psychologist nowadays would say, 'The feelings of my eyes or of my ears or of my skin'. People of course say that they have feelings in their big toe or ear, but no scientific language of that kind is possible any more. Taking those two words as identical, one could express the most exalted moods by the word Empfindung, but it is exactly as if a Frenchman spoke of 'les sensations les plus nobles de l'amour'. People would laugh, you know. It would be absolutely impossible, shocking!

Dr E. A. Bennet:

Do you consider that the superior function in the case of a person suffering from manic-depression remains conscious during the period of depression?

Professor Jung:

I would not say that. If you consider the case of manic-depressive insanity you occasionally find that in the manic phase one function prevails and in the depressive phase another function prevails. For instance, people who are lively, sanguine, nice and kind in the manic phase, and do not think very much, suddenly become very thoughtful when the depression comes on, and then they have obsessive thoughts, and vice versa. I know several cases of intellectuals who have a manic-depressive disposition. In the manic phase they think freely, they are productive and very clear and very abstract. Then the depressive phase comes on, and they have obsessive feelings; they are obsessed by terrible moods, just moods, not thoughts. Those are, of course, psychological details.

You see these things most clearly in cases of men of forty and a little bit more who have led a particular type of life, an intellectual life or a life of values, and suddenly that thing goes under and up comes just the contrary. There are very interesting cases like that. We have the famous literary illustrations, Nietzsche for instance. He is a most impressive example of a change of psychology into its opposite at middle age. In younger years he was the aphorist in the French style; in later years, at 38, in *Thus Spake Zarathustra*, he burst out in a Dionysian mood which was absolutely the contrary of everything he had written before.

Dr Bennet:

Is melancholia not extroverted?

Professor Jung:

You cannot say that, because it is an incommensurable consideration. Melancholia in itself could be termed an introverted condition but it is not an attitude of preference. When you call somebody an introvert, you mean that he prefers an introverted habit, but he has his extroverted side too. We all have both sides, otherwise we could not adapt at all, we would have no influence, we would be beside ourselves. Depression is always an introverted condition. Melancholics sink down into a sort of embryonic condition, therefore you find that accumulation of peculiar physical symptoms.

Dr Mary C. Luff:

As Professor Jung has explained emotion as an obsessive thing which possesses the individual, I am not clear how he differentiates what he calls 'invasions' from 'affects'.

Professor Jung:

You experience sometimes what you call 'pathological' emotions, and there you observe most peculiar contents coming through as emotion: thoughts you have never thought before, sometimes terrible thoughts and fantasies. For instance, some people when they are very angry, instead of having the ordinary feelings of revenge and so on, have the most terrific fantasies of committing murder, cutting off the arms and legs of the enemy, and such things. Those are invading fragments of the unconscious, and if you take a fully developed pathological emotion it is really a state of *eclipse* of consciousness when people are raving mad for a while and do perfectly crazy things. That is an invasion. That would be a pathological case, but fantasies of this kind can also occur within the limits of normal. I have heard innocent people say, 'I could cut him limb from limb', and they actually do have these bloody fantasies; they would 'smash the brains' of people, they imagine doing what in cold blood is merely *said* as a metaphor. When these fantasies get vivid and people are afraid of themselves, you speak of invasion.

Dr Luff:

Is that what you call confusional psychosis?

Professor Jung:

It does not need to be a psychosis at all. It does not need to be pathological; you can observe such things in normal people when they are under the sway of a particular emotion. I once went through a very strong earthquake. It was the first time in my life I experienced an earthquake. I was simply overcome by the idea that the earth was not solid and that it was the skin of a huge animal that had shaken itself as a horse does. I was simply caught by that idea for a while. Then I came out of the fantasy remembering that that is exactly what the Japanese say about earthquakes: that the big salamander has turned over or changed its position, the salamander that is carrying the earth.[17] Then I was satisfied that it was an archaic idea which had jumped into my consciousness. I thought it was remarkable; I did not quite think it was pathological.

Dr B. D. Hendy:

Would Professor Jung say that affect, as he defined it, is *caused* by a characteristic physiological condition, or would he say that this physiological alteration is the *result* of, let us say, invasion?

Professor Jung:

The relation between body and mind is a very difficult question. You know that the James-Lange theory says that affect is the result of physiological alteration. The question whether the body or the mind is the predominating factor will always be answered according to temperamental differences. Those who by temperament prefer the theory of the supremacy of the body will say that mental processes are epiphenomena of physiological chemistry. Those who believe more in the spirit will say the contrary, to them the body is just the appendix of the mind and causation lies with the spirit. It is really a philosophical question, and since I am not a philosopher I cannot claim to make a decision. All we can know empirically is that processes of the body and processes of the mind happen together in some way which is mysterious to us. It is due to our most lamentable mind that we cannot think of body and mind as one and the same thing; probably they *are* one thing, but we are unable to think it. Modern physics is subject to the same difficulty; look at the regrettable things which happen with light! Light behaves as if it were oscillations, and it also behaves as if it were corpuscles. It needed a very complicated mathematical formula by M. de Broglie to help the human mind to conceive the possibility that oscillations and corpuscles are two phenomena, observed under different conditions, of one and the same ultimate reality.[18] You cannot think this, but you are forced to admit it as a postulate.

In the same way, the so-called psychophysical parallelism is an insoluble problem. Take for instance the case of typhoid fever with psychological concomitants. If the psychic factor were mistaken for a causation, you would reach preposterous conclusions. All we can say is that there are certain physiological conditions which are clearly caused by mental disorder, and certain others which are not caused but merely accompanied by psychic processes. Body and mind are the two aspects of the living being, and that is all we know. Therefore I prefer to say that the two things happen together in a miraculous way, and we had better leave it at that, because we cannot think of them together. For my own use I have coined a term to illustrate this being together; I say there is a peculiar principle of synchronicity[19] active in the world so that things happen together somehow and behave as if they were the same, and yet for us they are not. Perhaps we shall some day discover a new kind of mathematical method by which we can prove that it must be like that. But for the time being I am absolutely unable to tell you whether it is the body or the mind that prevails, or whether they just coexist.

Dr L. J. Bendit:

I am not quite clear when invasion becomes pathological. You suggested in the first part of your talk this evening that invasion became pathological whenever it became habitual. What is the difference between a pathological invasion and an artistic inspiration and creation of ideas?

Professor Jung:

Between an artistic inspiration and an invasion there is absolutely no difference. It is exactly the same, therefore I avoid the word 'pathological'. I would never say that artistic inspiration is pathological, and therefore I make that exception for invasions too, because I consider that an inspiration is a perfectly normal fact. There is nothing bad in it. It is nothing out of the ordinary. Happily enough it belongs to the order of human beings that inspiration takes place occasionally – very rarely, but it does. But it is quite certain that pathological things come in pretty much the same way, so we have to draw the line somewhere. If you are all alienists and I present to you a certain case, then you might say that that man is insane. I would say that that man is not insane for this reason, that as long as he can explain himself to me in such a way that I feel I have a contact with him that man is not crazy. To be crazy is a very relative conception. For instance, when a Negro behaves in a certain way we say, 'Oh well, he's only a Negro', but if a white man behaves in the same way we say, 'That man is crazy', because a white man cannot behave like that. A Negro is expected to do such things but a white man does not do them. To be 'crazy' is a social concept; we use social restrictions and definitions in order to distinguish mental disturbances. You can say that a man is peculiar, that he behaves in an unexpected way and has funny ideas, and if he happens to live in a little town in France or Switzerland you would say, 'He is an original fellow, one of the most original inhabitants of that little place'; but if you bring that man into the midst of Harley Street, well, he is plumb crazy. Or if a certain individual is a painter, you think he is a very original artist, but let that man be the cashier of a big bank and the bank will experience something. Then they will say that fellow is surely crazy. But these are simply social considerations. We see the same thing in lunatic asylums. It is not an absolute increase in insanity that makes our asylums swell like monsters, it is the fact that we cannot stand abnormal people any more, so there are apparently very many more crazy people than formerly. I remember in my youth we had people whom I recognized later on as being schizophrenic, and we thought, 'Well, Uncle So-and-So is a very original man'. In my native town we had some imbeciles, but one did not say, 'He is a terrible ass', or something like that, but 'He is very nice'. In the same way one called certain idiots 'cretins', which comes from the saying 'il est bon chrétien'. You could not say anything else of them, but at least they were good Christians.

The Chairman:

Ladies and Gentlemen, I think we must let Professor Jung off any further activity for tonight, and we thank him very much indeed.

NOTES

1 [*Anthropologie in pragmatischer Hinsicht* (1798), Pt. I, Bk. I, sec. 5.]

2 ['There is nothing in the mind that was not in the senses'. Cf. Leibniz, *Nouveaux Essais sur l'Entendement humain*, Bk. II, ch. 1, sec. 2, in response to Locke. The formula was scholastic in origin; cf. Duns Scotus, *Super universalibus Porphyrii*, qu. 3.]

3 [*In Johannis Evang.*, XXXIV, 2. Cf. *Symbols of Transformation* (C.W., vol. 5), par. 162 and n. 69.]

4 [Cf. 'The Realities of Practical Psychotherapy' (C.W., vol. 16, 2nd edn.), pars. 558 ff.]

5 [What Jung may have had in mind are the *melothesiae*, explained in 'Psychology and Religion' (C.W., vol. 11), par. 113, n. 5; cf. *Psychology and Alchemy*, fig. 156.]

6 [*Psychological Types* (C.W., vol. 6), Definition 47.]

7 [Ibid., Def. 53.]

8 [Ibid., Def. 5.]

9   [Ibid., Def. 21 (1923 edn., Def. 20).]
10 [Ibid., Def. 44.]
11 [Ibid., Def. 35.]
12 [Ibid., Def. 30.]
13 [Ibid.]
14 [The theory was independently advanced by William James and by the Danish physiologist C. G. Lange, and is commonly referred to by both their names.]
15 [Jung and Peterson, 'Psychophysical Investigations with the Galvanometer and Pneumograph in Normal and Insane Individuals' (1907); Jung and Ricksher, 'Further Investigations on the Galvanic Phenomenon and Respiration in Normal and Insane Individuals' (1907). Both to be republished in *Experimental Researches* (C.W., vol. 2).]
16 [Possibly a stenographic slip for Jakob Freundlich, who conducted electro-cardiogram experiments; see his article in *Deutsches Archiv für klinische Medizin* (Berlin), 177:4 (1934).]
17 [According to a Japanese legend, the *namazu*, a kind of catfish of monstrous size, carries on its back most of Japan, and when annoyed it moves its head or tail, thus provoking earthquakes. The legend is often depicted in Japanese art.]
18 [Louis Victor de Broglie, French physicist, recipient of Nobel prize for physics (1929), discovered the wave character of electrons. Instead of 'oscillations' and 'corpuscles', the more usual terms here would be 'waves' and 'particles'.]
19 [Cf. 'Synchronicity: An Acausal Connecting Principle' (C.W., vol. 8).]

LECTURE TWO

The Chairman (Dr J. A. Hadfield):

Ladies and Gentlemen, you have already been introduced to Dr Jung and that in the most eulogistic language, but I think all who were here last night will recognize that even such a great eulogy was in no sense exaggerated. Dr Jung last night was referring to a number of the functions of the human mind, such as feeling, thinking, intuition, and sensation, and I could not help feeling that in him all these functions, contrary to what he told us, seemed to be very well differentiated. I also had a hunch that in him they were bound together in the centre by a sense of humour. Nothing convinces me so much of the truth of any conception as when its creator is able to see it as a subject of humour, and that is what Dr Jung did last night. Overseriousness in regard to any subject very often displays the fact that the individual is dubious and anxious about the truth of what he is trying to convey.

Professor Jung:

Ladies and Gentlemen, yesterday we dealt with the functions of consciousness. Today I want to finish the problem of the structure of the mind. A discussion of the human mind would not be complete if we did not include the existence of unconscious processes. Let me repeat shortly the reflections which I made last night.

   We cannot deal with unconscious processes directly because they are not reachable. They are not directly apprehended; they appear only in their products, and we postulate from the peculiar quality of those products that there must be something behind them from which they originate. We call that dark sphere the unconscious psyche.

The ectopsychic contents of consciousness derive in the first place from the environment, through the data of the senses. Then the contents also come from other sources, such as memory and processes of judgment. These belong to the endopsychic sphere. A third source for conscious contents is the dark sphere of the mind, the unconscious. We approach it through the peculiarities of the endopsychic functions, those functions which are not under the control of the will. They are the vehicle by which unconscious contents reach the surface of consciousness.

The unconscious processes, then, are not directly observable, but those of its products that cross the threshold of consciousness can be divided into two classes. The first class contains recognizable material of a definitely personal origin; these contents are individual acquisitions or products of instinctive processes that make up the personality as a whole. Furthermore, there are forgotten or repressed contents, and creative contents. There is nothing specially peculiar about them. In other people such things may be conscious. Some people are conscious of things of which other people are not. I call that class of contents the subconscious mind or the *personal unconscious*, because, as far as we can judge, it is entirely made up of personal elements, elements that constitute the human personality as a whole.

Then there is another class of contents of definitely unknown origin, or at all events of an origin which cannot be ascribed to individual acquisition. These contents have one outstanding peculiarity, and that is their mythological character. It is as if they belong to a pattern not peculiar to any particular mind or person, but rather to a pattern peculiar to *mankind in general*. When I first came across such contents I wondered very much whether they might not be due to heredity, and I thought they might be explained by racial inheritance. In order to settle that question I went to the United States and studied the dreams of pure-blooded Negroes, and I was able to satisfy myself that these images have nothing to do with so-called blood or racial inheritance, nor are they personally acquired by the individual. They belong to mankind in general, and therefore they are of a *collective* nature.

These collective patterns I have called *archetypes*, using an expression of St Augustine's.[1] An archetype means a *typos* [imprint], a definite grouping of archaic character containing, in form as well as in meaning, *mythological motifs*. Mythological motifs appear in pure form in fairytales, myths, legends, and folklore. Some of the well-known motifs are: the figures of the Hero, the Redeemer, the Dragon (always connected with the Hero, who has to overcome him), the Whale or the Monster who swallows the Hero.[2] Another variation of the motif of the Hero and the Dragon is the Katabasis, the Descent into the Cave, the Nekyia. You remember in the Odyssey where Ulysses descends *ad inferos* to consult Tiresias, the seer. This motif of the Nekyia is found everywhere in antiquity and practically all over the world. It expresses the psychological mechanism of introversion of the conscious mind into the deeper layers of the unconscious psyche. From these layers derive the contents of an impersonal, mythological character, in other words, the archetypes, and I call them therefore the impersonal or *collective unconscious*.

I am perfectly well aware that I can give you only the barest outline of this particular question of the collective unconscious. But I will give you an example of its symbolism and of how I proceed in order to discriminate it from the personal unconscious. When I went to America to investigate the unconscious of Negroes I had in mind this particular problem: are these collective patterns racially inherited, or are they 'a priori categories of imagination', as two Frenchmen, Hubert and Mauss,[3] quite independently of my own work, have called them. A Negro told me a dream in which occurred the figure of a man crucified on a wheel.[4] I will not mention the whole dream because it does not matter. It contained of course its personal meaning as well as allusions to impersonal ideas, but I picked out only that one motif. He was a very uneducated Negro from the South and not particularly intelligent. It would have been most probable, given the well-known religious character of the Negroes, that he should dream of a man crucified on a *cross*. The cross would have been a personal acquisition. But it is rather improbable that he should dream of the man crucified on a *wheel*. That is a very uncommon image. Of course I cannot prove to you that by some curious chance the Negro had not seen a picture or heard something of the sort and then dreamt about it; but if he had not had any model for this idea it would be an *archetypal image*, because the crucifixion on the wheel is a *mythological motif*. It is the ancient sun-wheel, and the crucifixion is the sacrifice to the sun-god in order to propitiate him, just as human and animal sacrifices formerly were offered for the fertility of the earth. The sun-wheel is an exceedingly archaic idea, perhaps the oldest religious idea there is. We can trace it to the Mesolithic and Paleolithic ages, as the sculptures of Rhodesia prove. Now there were real wheels only in the Bronze Age; in the Paleolithic Age the wheel was not yet invented. The Rhodesian sun-wheel seems to be contemporary with very naturalistic animal-pictures, like the famous rhino with the tick-birds, a masterpiece of observation. The Rhodesian sun-wheel is therefore an original vision, presumably an archetypal sun-image.[5] But this image is not a naturalistic one, for it is always divided into four or eight partitions (Figure 3). This image, a sort of divided circle, is a symbol which you find throughout the whole history of mankind as well as in the dreams of modern individuals. We might assume that the invention of the actual wheel started from this vision. Many of our inventions came from mythological anticipations and primordial images. For instance, the art of alchemy is the

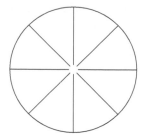

Figure 3 Sun-wheel

mother of modern chemistry. Our conscious scientific mind started in the matrix of the unconscious mind.

In the dream of the Negro, the man on the wheel is a repetition of the Greek mythological motif of Ixion, who, on account of his offence against men and gods, was fastened by Zeus upon an incessantly turning wheel. I give you this example of a mythological motif in a dream merely in order to convey to you an idea of the collective unconscious. One single example is of course no conclusive proof. But one cannot very well assume that this Negro had studied Greek mythology, and it is improbable that he had seen any representation of Greek mythological figures. Furthermore, figures of Ixion are pretty rare.

I could give you conclusive proof of a very elaborate kind of the existence of these mythological patterns in the unconscious mind. But in order to present my material I should need to lecture for a fortnight. I would have first to explain to you the meaning of dreams and dream-series and then give you all the historical parallels and explain fully their importance, because the symbolism of these images and ideas is not taught in public schools or universities, and even specialists very rarely know of it. I had to study it for years and to find the material myself, and I cannot expect even a highly educated audience to be *au courant* with such abstruse matters. When we come to the technique of dream-analysis I shall be forced to enter into some of the mythological material and you will get a glimpse of what this work of finding parallels to unconscious products is really like. For the moment I have to content myself with the mere statement that there are mythological patterns in that layer of the unconscious, that it produces contents which cannot be ascribed to the individual and which may even be in strict contradiction to the personal psychology of the dreamer. For instance, you are simply astounded when you observe a completely uneducated person producing a dream which really should not occur with such a person because it contains the most amazing things. And children's dreams often make you think to such a degree that you must take a holiday afterwards in order to recover from the shock, because these symbols are so tremendously profound, and you think: How on earth is it possible that a child should have such a dream?

It is really quite simple to explain. Our mind has its history, just as our body has its history. You might be just as astonished that man has an appendix, for instance. Does he know he ought to have an appendix? He is just born with it. Millions of people do not know they have a thymus, but they have it. They do not know that in certain parts of their anatomy they belong to the species of the fishes, and yet it is so. Our unconscious mind, like our body, is a storehouse of relics and memories of the past. A study of the structure of the unconscious collective mind would reveal the same discoveries as you make in comparative anatomy. We do not need to think that there is anything mystical about it. But because I speak of a collective unconscious, I have been accused of obscurantism. There is nothing mystical about the collective unconscious. It is just a new branch of science, and it is really common sense to admit the existence of unconscious collective processes. For, though a child is not born conscious, his mind is not a *tabula rasa*. The child is born with a definite brain, and the brain of an English child will work not like that of an Australian blackfellow but in the way of a modern English person. The brain is born with a finished structure, it will work in a modern way, but this brain has its history. It has been built up in the course of millions of years and represents a history of which it is the result. Naturally it carries with it the traces of that history, exactly like the body, and if you grope down into the basic structure of the mind you naturally find traces of the archaic mind.

The idea of the collective unconscious is really very simple. If it were not so, then one could speak of a miracle, and I am not a miracle-monger at all. I simply go by experience. If I could tell you the experiences you would draw the same conclusions about these archaic motifs. By chance, I stumbled somehow into mythology and have read more books perhaps than you. I have not always been a student of mythology. One day, when I was still at the clinic, I saw a patient with schizophrenia who had a peculiar vision, and he told me about it. He wanted me to see it and, being very dull, I could not see it. I thought, 'This man is crazy and I am normal and his vision should not bother me'. But it did. I asked myself: What does it mean? I was not satisfied that it was just crazy, and later I came on a book by a German scholar, Dieterich,[6] who had published part of a magic papyrus. I studied it with great interest, and on page 7 I found the vision of my lunatic 'word for word'. That gave me a shock. I said: 'How on earth is it possible that this fellow came into possession of that vision?' It was not just one image, but a series of images and a literal repetition of them. I do not want to go into it now because it would lead us too far. It is a highly interesting case: as a matter of fact, I published it.[7]

This astonishing parallelism set me going. You probably have not come across the book of the learned professor Dieterich, but if you had read the same books and observed such cases you would have discovered the idea of the collective unconscious.

The deepest we can reach in our exploration of the unconscious mind is the layer where man is no longer a distinct individual, but where his mind widens out and merges into the mind of mankind – not the conscious mind, but the unconscious mind of mankind, where we are all the same. As the body has its anatomical conformity in its two eyes and two ears and one heart and so on, with only slight individual differences, so has the mind its basic conformity. On this collective level we are no longer separate individuals, we are all one. You can understand this when you study the psychology of primitives. The outstanding fact about the primitive mentality is this lack of distinctiveness between individuals, this oneness of the subject with the object, this *participation mystique* as Lévy-Bruhl[8] terms it. Primitive mentality expresses the basic structure of the mind, that psychological layer which with us is the collective unconscious, that underlying level which is the same in all. Because the basic structure of the mind is the same in everybody, we cannot make distinctions when we experience on that level. There we do not know if something has happened to you or to me. In the underlying collective level there is a wholeness which cannot be dissected. If you begin to think about participation as a fact which means that fundamentally we are identical with everybody and everything, you are led to very peculiar theoretical conclusions. You should not go further than those conclusions because these things get dangerous. But some of the conclusions you should explore, because they can explain a lot of peculiar things that happen to man.

I want to sum up: I have brought a diagram (Figure 4). It looks very complicated but as a matter of fact it is very simple. Suppose our mental sphere to look like a lighted globe. The surface from which the light emanates is the function by which you chiefly adapt. If you are a person who adapts chiefly by thinking, your surface is the surface of a thinking man. You will tackle things with your thinking, and what you will show to people will be your thinking. It will be another function if you are of another type.[9]

In the diagram, *sensation* is given as the peripheral function. By it man gets information from the world of external objects. In the second circle, *thinking*, he gets what his senses have told him; he will give things a name. Then he will have a *feeling* about them; a feeling-tone will accompany his observation. And in the end he will get some consciousness of where a thing comes from, where it may go, and what it may do. That is *intuition*, by which you see round corners. These four functions form the ectopsychic system.

The next sphere in the diagram represents the conscious ego-complex to which the functions refer. Inside the endopsyche you first notice *memory*, which is still a function that can be controlled by the will; it is under the control of your ego-complex. Then we meet the *subjective components of the functions*. They cannot be exactly directed by the will but they still can be suppressed, excluded, or increased in intensity by will-power. These components are no longer as controllable as memory, though even memory

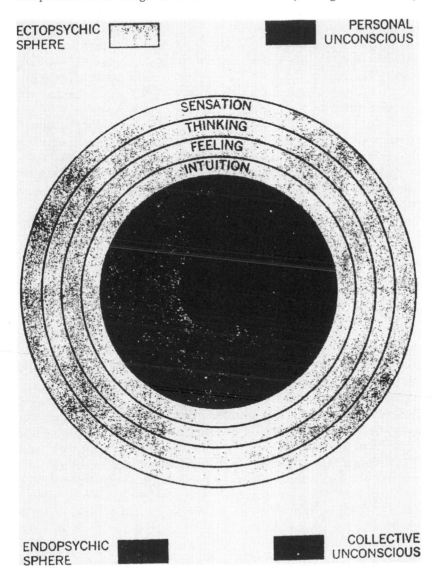

Figure 4 The Psyche

is a bit tricky as you know. Then we come to the *affects* and *invasions*, which are only controllable by sheer force. You can suppress them, and that is all you can do. You have to clench your fists in order not to explode because they are apt to be stronger than your ego-complex.

This psychic system cannot really be expressed by such a crude diagram. The diagram is rather a scale of values showing how the energy or intensity of the ego-complex which manifests itself in will-power gradually decreases as you approach the darkness that is ultimately at the bottom of the whole structure – the *unconscious*. First we have the personal subconscious mind. The *personal unconscious* is that part of the psyche which contains all the things that could just as well be conscious. You know that many things are termed unconscious, but that is only a relative statement. There is nothing in this particular sphere that is necessarily unconscious in everybody. There are people who are conscious of almost anything of which man can be conscious. Of course we have an extraordinary amount of unconsciousness in our civilization, but if you go to other races, to India or to China, for example, you discover that these people are conscious of things for which the psychoanalyst in our countries has to dig for months. Moreover, simple people in natural conditions often have an extraordinary consciousness of things of which people in towns have no knowledge and of which townspeople begin to dream only under the influence of psychoanalysis. I noticed this at school. I had lived in the country among peasants and with animals, and I was fully conscious of a number of things of which other boys had no idea. I had the chance and I was not prejudiced. When you analyse dreams or symptoms or fantasies of neurotic or normal people, you begin to penetrate the unconscious mind, and you can abolish its artificial threshold. The personal unconscious is really something very relative, and its circle can be restricted and become so much narrower that it touches zero. It is quite thinkable that a man can develop his consciousness to such an extent that he can say: *Nihil humanum a me alienum puto.*[10]

Finally we come to the ultimate kernel which cannot be made conscious at all – the sphere of the archetypal mind. Its presumable contents appear in the form of images which can be understood only by comparing them with historical parallels. If you do not recognize certain material as historical and if you do not possess the parallels, you cannot integrate these contents into consciousness and they remain projected. The contents of the *collective unconscious* are not subject to any arbitrary intention and are not controllable by the will. They actually behave as if they did not exist in yourself – you see them in your neighbours but not in yourself. When the contents of the collective unconscious become activated, we become aware of certain things in our fellow men. For instance, we begin to discover that the bad Abyssinians are attacking Italy. You know the famous story by Anatole France. Two peasants were always fighting each other, and there was somebody who wanted to go into the reasons for it, and he asked one man: 'Why do you hate your neighbour and fight him like this?' He replied: 'Mais il est de l'autre côté de la rivière!' That is like France and Germany. We Swiss people, you know, had a very good chance during the Great War to read newspapers and to study that particular mechanism which behaved like a great gun firing on one side of the Rhine and in exactly the same way on the other side, and it was very clear that people saw in their neighbours the thing they did not recognize in themselves.

As a rule, when the collective unconscious becomes really constellated in larger social groups, the result is a public craze, a mental epidemic that may lead to revolution or war or something of the sort. These movements are exceedingly contagious – almost overwhelmingly contagious because, when the collective unconscious is activated, you are no longer the same person. You are not only in the movement – you *are* it. If you lived in Germany or were there for a while, you would defend yourself in vain. It gets under your skin. You are human, and wherever you are in the world you can defend yourself only by restricting your consciousness and making yourself as empty, as soulless, as possible. Then you lose your soul, because you are only a speck of consciousness floating on a sea of life in which you do not participate. But if you remain yourself you will notice that the collective atmosphere gets under your skin. You cannot live in Africa or any such country without having that country under your skin. If you live with the yellow man you get yellow under the skin. You cannot prevent it, because somewhere you are the same as the Negro or the Chinese or whoever you live with, you are all just human beings. In the collective unconscious you are the same as a man of another race, you have the same archetypes, just as you have, like him, eyes, a heart, a liver, and so on. It does not matter that his skin is black. It matters to a certain extent, sure enough – he has probably a whole historical layer less than you. The different strata of the mind correspond to the history of the races.

If you study races as I have done you can make very interesting discoveries. You can make them, for instance, if you analyse North Americans. The American, on account of the fact that he lives on virgin soil, has the Red Indian in him. The Red man, even if he has never seen one, and the Negro, though he may be cast out and the tram-cars reserved for white men only, have got into the American and you will realize that he belongs to a partly coloured nation.[11] These things are wholly unconscious, and you can only talk to very enlightened people about them. It is just as difficult to talk to Frenchmen or Germans when you have to tell them why they are so much against each other.

A little while ago I had a nice evening in Paris. Some very cultivated men had invited me, and we had a pleasant conversation. They asked me about national differences, and I thought I would put my foot in it, so I said: 'What you value is *la clarté latine, la clarté de l'esprit latin*. That is because your thinking is inferior. The Latin thinker is inferior in comparison to the German thinker'. They cocked their ears, and I said: 'But your feeling is unsurpassable, it is absolutely differentiated'. They said: 'How is that?' I replied: 'Go to a café or a vaudeville or a place where you hear songs and stage-plays and you will notice a very peculiar phenomenon. There are any number of very grotesque and cynical things and then suddenly something sentimental happens. A mother loses her child, there is a lost love, or something marvellously patriotic, and you must weep. For you, the salt and the sugar have to go together. But a German can stand a whole evening of sugar only. The Frenchman must have some salt in it. You meet a man and say: *Enchanté de faire votre connaissance*. You are not *enchanté de faire sa connaissance* at all; you are really feeling: Oh go to the devil. But you are not disturbed, nor is he. But do not say to a German: *Enchanté de faire votre connaissance*, because he will believe it. A German will sell you a pair of sock-suspenders and not only expect, as is natural, to be paid for it. He also expects to be loved for it'.

The German nation is characterized by the fact that its feeling function is inferior, it is not differentiated. If you say that to a German he is offended. I should be offended too. He is very attached to what he calls *Gemütlichkeit*. A room full of smoke in which everybody loves everybody – that is *gemütlich* and that must not be disturbed. It has to be absolutely clear, just one note and no more. That is *la clarté germanique du sentiment*, and it is inferior. On the other hand, it is a gross offence to a Frenchman to say something paradoxical, because it is not clear. An English philosopher has said, 'A superior mind is never quite clear'. That is true, and also superior feeling is never quite clear. You will only enjoy a feeling that is above board when it is slightly doubtful, and a thought that does not have a slight contradiction in it is not convincing.

Our particular problem from now on will be: How can we approach the dark sphere of man? As I have told you, this is done by three methods of analysis: the word-association test, dream-analysis, and the method of active imagination. First of all I want to say something about *word-association tests*.[12] To many of you perhaps these seem old-fashioned, but since they are still being used I have to refer to them. I use this test now not with patients but with criminal cases.

The experiment is made – I am repeating well-known things – with a list of say a hundred words. You instruct the test person to react with the first word that comes into his mind as quickly as possible after having heard and understood the stimulus word. When you have made sure that the test person has understood what you mean you start the experiment. You mark the time of each reaction with a stop-watch. When you have finished the hundred words you do another experiment. You repeat the stimulus words and the test person has to reproduce his former answers. In certain places his memory fails and reproduction becomes uncertain or faulty. These mistakes are important.

Originally the experiment was not meant for its present application at all; it was intended to be used for the study of mental association. That was of course a most Utopian idea. One can study nothing of the sort by such primitive means. But you can study something else when the experiment fails, when people make mistakes. You ask a simple word that a child can answer, and a highly intelligent person cannot reply. Why? That word has hit on what I call a complex, a conglomeration of psychic contents characterized by a peculiar or perhaps painful feeling-tone, something that is usually hidden from sight. It is as though a projectile struck through the thick layer of the persona[13] into the dark layer. For instance, somebody with a money complex will be hit when you say: 'To buy', 'to pay', or 'money'. That is a disturbance of reaction.

We have about twelve or more categories of disturbance and I will mention a few of them so that you will get an idea of their practical value. The prolongation of the reaction time is of the greatest practical importance. You decide whether the reaction time is too long by taking the average mean of the reaction times of the test person. Other characteristic disturbances are: reaction with more than one word, against the instructions; mistakes in reproduction of the word; reaction expressed by facial expression, laughing, movement of the hands or feet or body, coughing, stammering, and such things; insufficient reactions like 'yes' or 'no'; not reacting to the real meaning of the stimulus word; habitual use of the same words; use of foreign languages – of which there is not a great danger in England, though with us it is a great nuisance; defective reproduction, when memory begins to fail in the reproduction experiment; total lack of reaction.

All these reactions are beyond the control of the will. If you submit to the experiment you are done for, and if you do not submit to it you are done for too, because one knows why you are unwilling to do so. If you put it to a criminal he can refuse, and that is fatal because one knows why he refuses. If he gives in he hangs himself. In Zurich I am called in by the Court when they have a difficult case; I am the last straw.

The results of the association test can be illustrated very neatly by a diagram (Figure 5). The height of the columns represents the actual reaction time of the test person. The dotted horizontal line represents the average mean of reaction times. The unshaded columns are those reactions which show no signs of disturbance. The shaded columns show disturbed reactions. In reactions 7, 8, 9, 10, you observe for instance a whole series of disturbances: the stimulus word at 7 was a critical one, and without the test person noticing it at all three subsequent reaction times are overlong on account of the perseveration of the reaction to the stimulus word. The test person was

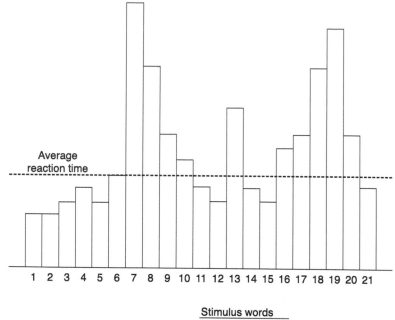

Average reaction time

1 2 3 4 5 6 7 8 9 10 11 12 13 14 15 16 17 18 19 20 21

Stimulus words

7 knife
13 lance (= spear)
16 to beat
18 pointed
19 bottle

Figure 5 Association Test

quite unconscious of the fact that he had an emotion. Reaction 13 shows an isolated disturbance, and in 16–20 the result is again a whole series of disturbances. The strongest disturbances are in reactions 18 and 19. In this particular case we have to do with a so-called intensification of sensitiveness through the sensitizing effect of an unconscious emotion: when a critical stimulus word has aroused a perseverating emotional reaction, and when the next critical stimulus word happens to occur within the range of that perseveration, then it is apt to produce a greater effect than it would have been expected to produce if it had occurred in a series of indifferent associations. This is called the sensitizing effect of a perseverating emotion.

In dealing with criminal cases we can make use of the sensitizing effect, and then we arrange the critical stimulus words in such a way that they occur more or less within the presumable range of perseveration. This can be done in order to increase the effect of critical stimulus words. With a suspected culprit as a test person, the critical stimulus words are words which have a direct bearing upon the crime.

The test person for Figure 5 was a man about 35, a decent individual, one of my normal test persons. I had of course to experiment with a great number of normal people before I could draw conclusions from pathological material. If you want to know what it was that disturbed this man, you simply have to read the words that caused the disturbances and fit them together. Then you get a nice story. I will tell you exactly what it was.

To begin with, it was the word *knife* that caused four disturbed reactions. The next disturbance was *lance* (or *spear*) and then *to beat*, then the word *pointed* and then *bottle*. That was in a short series of fifty stimulus words, which was enough for me to tell the man point-blank what the matter was. So I said: 'I did not know you had had such a disagreeable experience'. He stared at me and said: 'I do not know what you are talking about'. I said, 'You know you were drunk and had a disagreeable affair with sticking your knife into somebody'. He said: 'How do you know?' Then he confessed the whole thing. He came of a respectable family, simple but quite nice people. He had been abroad and one day got into a drunken quarrel, drew a knife and stuck it into somebody, and got a year in prison. That is a great secret which he does not mention because it would cast a shadow on his life. Nobody in his town or surroundings knows anything about it and I am the only one who by chance stumbled upon it. In my seminar in Zurich I also make these experiments. Those who want to confess are of course welcome to. However, I always ask them to bring some material of a person they know and I do not know, and I show them how to read the story of that individual. It is quite interesting work; sometimes one makes remarkable discoveries.

I will give you other instances. Many years ago, when I was quite a young doctor, an old professor of criminology asked me about the experiment and said he did not believe in it. I said: 'No, Professor? You can try it whenever you like'. He invited me to his house and I began. After ten words he got tired and said: 'What can you make of it? Nothing has come of it'. I told him he could not expect a result with ten or twelve words; he ought to have a hundred and then we would see something. He said: 'Can you do something with these words?' I said: 'Little enough, but I can tell you something. Quite recently you have had worries about money, you have too little of it. You are afraid of dying of heart disease. You must have studied in France, where you had a love affair, and it has come back to your mind, as often, when one has thoughts of dying, old sweet memories come back from the womb of time'. He said: 'How do you know?' Any child could have seen it! He was a man of 72 and he had associated *heart* with *pain* – fear that he would die of heart failure. He associated *death* with *to die* – a natural reaction – and with *money* he associated *too little*, a very usual reaction. Then things became rather startling to me. To *pay*, after a long reaction time, he said *La Semeuse*, though our conversation was in German. That is the famous figure on the French coin. Now why on earth should this old man say *La Semeuse?* When he came to the word *kiss* there was a long reaction time and there was a light in his eyes and he said: *Beautiful.* Then of course I had the story. He would never have used French if it had not been associated with a particular feeling, and so we must think why he used it. Had he had losses with the French franc? There was no talk of inflation and devaluation in those days. That could not be the clue. I was in doubt whether it was money or love, but when he came to *kiss/beautiful* I knew it was love. He was not the kind of man to go to France in later life, but he had been a student in Paris, a lawyer, probably at the Sorbonne. It was relatively simple to stitch together the whole story.

But occasionally you come upon a real tragedy. Figure 6 is the case of a woman of about thirty years of age. She was in the clinic, and the diagnosis was schizophrenia of a depressive character. The prognosis was correspondingly bad. I had this woman in my ward, and I had a peculiar feeling about her. I felt I could not quite agree with the bad prognosis, because already schizophrenia was a relative idea with me. I thought that we are all relatively crazy, but this woman was peculiar, and I could not accept the diagnosis as the last word. In those days one knew precious little. Of course I made an anamnesis, but nothing was discovered that threw any light on her illness. Therefore I put her to the association test and finally made a very peculiar discovery. The first disturbance was caused by the word *angel*, and a complete lack of reaction by the word *obstinate.* Then there were *evil*, *rich*, *money*, *stupid*, *dear*, and *to marry*. Now this woman was the wife of a well-to-do man in a very fine position and apparently happy. I had questioned her husband, and the only thing he could tell me, as she also did, was that the depression came on about two months after her eldest child had died – a little girl four years old. Nothing else could be found out about the aetiology of the case. The association test confronted me with a most baffling series of reactions which I could not put together. You will often be in such a situation, particularly if you have no routine with that kind of diagnosis. Then you first ask the test person about the words which are not going directly to the kernel. If you asked directly about the strongest disturbances you would get wrong answers, so you begin with relatively harmless words and you are likely to get an honest reply. I said: 'What about *angel*? Does that word mean something to you?' She replied: 'Of course, that is my child whom I have lost'. And then came a great flood of tears. When the storm had blown over I asked: 'What does *obstinate* mean to you?' She said: 'It means nothing to me'. But I said: 'There was a big disturbance with the word and it means there is something connected with it'. I could not

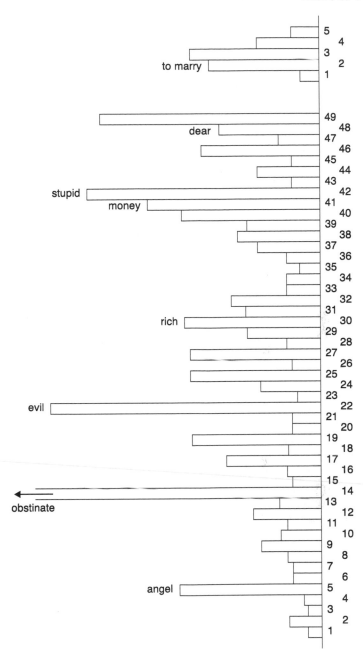

Figure 6 Association Test

penetrate it. I came to the word *evil* and could get nothing out of her. There was a severely negative reaction which showed that she refused to answer. I went on to *blue*, and she said: 'Those are the eyes of the child I have lost'. I said: 'Did they make a particular impression on you?' She said: 'Of course. They were so wonderfully blue when the child was born'. I noticed the expression on her face, and I said: 'Why are you upset?' and she replied: 'Well, she did not have the eyes of my husband'. Finally it came out that the child had had the eyes of a former lover of hers. I said: 'What is upsetting you with regard to that man?' And I was able to worm the story out of her.

In the little town in which she grew up there was a rich young man. She was of a well-to-do family but nothing grand. The man was of the moneyed aristocracy and the hero of the little town, and every girl dreamed of him. She was a pretty girl and thought she might have a chance. Then she discovered she had no chance with him, and her family said: 'Why think of him? He is a rich man and does not think of you. Here is Mr So-and-So, a nice man. Why not marry him?' She married him and was perfectly happy ever after until the fifth year of her marriage, when a former friend from her native town came to visit her. When her husband left the room he said to her: 'You have caused pain to a certain gentleman' (meaning the hero). She said: 'What? I caused pain?' The friend replied: 'Didn't you know he was in love with you and was disappointed when you married another man?' That set fire to the roof. But she repressed it. A fortnight later she was bathing her boy, two years, and her girl, four years old. The water in the town – it was not in Switzerland – was not above suspicion, in fact it was infected with typhoid fever. She noticed that the little girl was sucking a sponge. But she did not interfere, and when the little boy said, 'I want to drink some water', she gave him the possibly infected water. The little girl got typhoid fever and died, the little boy was saved. Then she had what she wanted – or what the devil in her wanted – the denial of her marriage in order to marry the other man. To this end she had committed murder. She did not know it: she only told me the facts and did not draw the conclusion that she was responsible for the death of the child since she knew the water was infected and there was danger. I was faced with the question whether I should tell her she had committed murder, or whether I should keep quiet. (It was only a question of telling *her*, there was no threat of a criminal case.) I thought that if I told her it might make her condition much worse, but there was a bad prognosis anyhow, whereas, if she could realize what she had done, the chance was that she might get well. So I made up my mind to tell her point-blank: 'You killed your child'. She went up in the air in an emotional state, but then she came down to the facts. In three weeks we were able to discharge her, and she never came back. I traced her for fifteen years, and there was no relapse. That depression fitted her case psychologically: she was a murderess and under other circumstances would have deserved capital punishment. Instead of going to jail she was sent to the lunatic asylum. I practically saved her from the punishment of insanity by putting an enormous burden on her conscience. For if one can accept one's sin one can live with it. If one cannot accept it, one has to suffer the inevitable consequences.

DISCUSSION

Question:

I want to refer to last night. Towards the end of his lecture Dr Jung spoke of higher and lower functions and said the thinking type would use his feeling function archaically. I would like to know: is the reverse true? Does the feeling type, when he tries to think, think archaically? In other words, are thinking and intuition to be regarded always as higher functions than feeling and sensation? I ask this because . . . I gathered from lectures elsewhere that sensation was the lowest of conscious functions and thinking a higher one. It is certainly the case that in everyday life thinking seems to be the top-notch. The professor – not this Professor – thinking in his study regards himself and is regarded as the highest type, higher than the countryman who says: 'Sometimes I sits and thinks and sometimes I just sits.'

Professor Jung:

I hope I did not give you the impression that I was giving a preference to any of the functions. The dominating function in a given individual is always the most differentiated, and that can be any function. We have absolutely no criterion by which we can say this or that function in itself is the best. We can only say that the differentiated function in the individual is the best for adapting, and that the one that is most excluded by the superior function is inferior on account of being neglected. There are some modern people who say that intuition is the highest function. Fastidious individuals prefer intuition, it is classy! The sensation type always thinks that other people are very inferior because they are not so real as he is. He is the real fellow and everybody else is fantastic and unreal. Everybody thinks his superior function is the top of the world. In that respect we are liable to the most awful blunders. To realize the actual order of functions in our consciousness, severe psychological criticism is needed. There are many people who believe that world problems are settled by thinking. But no truth can be established without all four functions. When you have thought the world you have done one-fourth of it; the remaining three-fourths may be against you.

Dr Eric B. Strauss:

Professor Jung said the word-association test was a means by which one could study the contents of the personal unconscious. In the examples he gave surely the matters revealed were matters in the patient's conscious mind and not in his unconscious. Surely if one wanted to seek for unconscious material one would have to go a step further and get the patient to associate freely on the anomalous reactions. I am thinking of the association with the word 'knife', when Professor Jung so cleverly assumed the story of the unfortunate incident. That surely was in the patient's conscious mind, whereas, if the word 'knife' had unconscious associations we might, if we were Freudian-minded, have assumed it was associated with an unconscious castration complex or something of that kind. I am not saying it is so, but I do not understand what Professor Jung means when he says the association test is to reach to the patient's unconscious. Surely in the instance given tonight it is used to reach the conscious, or what Freud would perhaps call the preconscious.

Professor Jung:

I should like very much if you would pay more attention to what I say. I told you that unconscious things are very *relative*. When I am unconscious of a certain thing I am only relatively unconscious of it; in some other respects I may know it. The contents of the personal unconscious are perfectly conscious in certain respects, but you do not know them under a *particular aspect* or at a *particular time*.

How can you establish whether the thing is conscious or unconscious? You simply ask people. We have no other criterion to establish whether something is conscious or unconscious. You ask: 'Do you know whether you have had certain hesitations?' They say: 'No, I had no hesitation; to my knowledge I had the same reaction time'. 'Are you conscious that something disturbed you?' 'No, I am not'. 'Have you no recollection of what you answered to the word, "knife"?' 'None at all'. This unawareness of facts is a very common thing. When I am asked if I know a certain man I may say no, because I have no recollection of him and so I am not conscious of knowing him; but when I am told that I met him two years ago, that he is Mr So-and-So who has done such and such a thing, I reply: 'Certainly I know him'. I know him and I do not know him. All the contents of the personal unconscious are *relatively* unconscious, even the castration complex and the incest complex. They are perfectly known under certain aspects, though they are unconscious under others. This relativity of being conscious of something becomes quite plain in hysterical cases. Quite often you find that things which seem unconscious are unconscious only to the doctor but not perhaps to the nurse or the relatives.

I had to see an interesting case once in a famous clinic in Berlin, a case of multiple sarcomatosis of the spinal cord, and because it was a very famous neurologist who had made the diagnosis I almost trembled, but I asked for the anamnesis and had a very nice one worked out. I asked when the symptoms began, and found it was the evening of the day when the only son of the woman had left her and married. She was a widow, quite obviously in love with her son, and I said: 'This is no sarcomatosis but an ordinary hysteria, which we can prove presently'. The professor was horrified at my lack of intelligence or tact or I don't know what, and I had to walk out. But somebody ran after me in the street. It was the nurse, who said: 'Doctor, I want to thank you for saying that it *was* hysteria. I always thought so'.

Dr Eric Graham Howe:

May I return to what Dr Strauss said? Last night Professor Jung reproved me for merely using words, but I think it is important to get these words clearly understood. I wonder if you have ever asked for the association experiment to be applied to the words 'mystic' or 'fourth dimension'? I believe you would get a period of great delay and concentrated fury every time they were mentioned. I propose to return to the fourth-dimensional, because I believe it is a link badly needed to help our understanding. Dr Strauss uses the word 'unconscious', but I understand from Professor Jung that there is no such thing, there is only a relative unconsciousness which depends on a relative degree of consciousness. According to Freudians, there is a place, a thing, an entity called the unconscious. According to Professor Jung, as I understand him, there is no such thing. He is moving in a fluid medium of relationship and Freud in a static medium of unrelated entities. To get it clear Freud is three-dimensional and Jung is, in all his psychology, four-dimensional. For this reason, I would criticize if I may the whole diagrammatic system of Jung because he is giving you a three-dimensional presentation of a four-dimensional system, a static presentation of something that is functionally moving, and unless it is explained you get it confused with the Freudian terminology and you cannot understand it. I shall insist that there must be some clarification of words.

Professor Jung:

I could wish Dr Graham Howe were not so indiscreet. You are right, but you should not say such things. As I explained, I tried to begin with the mildest propositions. You put your foot right into it and speak of four dimensions and of the word 'mystic', and you tell me that all of us would have a long reaction time to such stimulus words. You are quite right, everybody would be stung because we are just beginners in our field. I agree with you that it is very difficult to let psychology be a living thing and not to dissolve it into static entities. Naturally you must express yourself in terms of the fourth dimension when you bring the time factor into a three-dimensional system. When you speak of dynamics and processes you need the time factor, and then you have all the prejudice of the world against you because you have used the word 'four-dimensional'. It is a taboo word that should not be mentioned. It has a history, and we should be exceedingly tactful with such words. The more you advance in the understanding of the psyche the more careful you will have to be with terminology, because it is historically coined and prejudiced. The more you penetrate the basic problems of psychology the more you approach ideas which are philosophically, religiously, and morally prejudiced. Therefore certain things should be handled with the utmost care.

Dr Howe:

This audience would like you to be provocative. I am going to say a rash thing. You and I do not regard the shape of the ego as a straight line. We would be prepared to regard the sphere as a true shape of the self in four dimensions, of which one is the three-dimensional outline. If so, will you answer a question. 'What is the scope of that self which in four dimensions is a moving sphere?' I suggest the answer is: 'The universe itself, which includes your concept of the collective racial unconscious'.

Professor Jung:

I should be much obliged if you would repeat that question.

Dr Howe:

How big is this sphere, which is the four-dimensional self? I could not help giving the answer and saying that it is the same bigness as the universe.

Professor Jung:

This is really a philosophical question, and to answer it requires a great deal of theory of cognition. The world is our picture. Only childish people imagine that the world is what we think it is. The image of the world is a projection of the world of the self, as the latter is an introjection of the world. But only the special mind of a philosopher will step beyond the ordinary picture of the world in which there are static and isolated things. If you stepped beyond that picture you would cause an earthquake in the ordinary mind, the whole cosmos would be shaken, the most sacred convictions and hopes would be upset, and I do not see why one should wish to disquiet things. It is not good for patients, nor for doctors; it is perhaps good for philosophers.

Dr Ian Suttie:

I should like to go back to Dr Strauss's question. I can understand what Dr Strauss means and I think I can understand what Professor Jung means. As far as I can see, Professor Jung fails to make any link between his statement and Dr Strauss's. Dr Strauss wanted to know how the word-association test can show the Freudian unconscious, the material that is actually pushed out of mind. As far as I understand Professor Jung, he means what Freud means by the 'Id'. It seems to me that we should define our ideas well enough to compare them and not merely use them, each in our own school.

Professor Jung:

I must repeat again that my methods do not discover theories, they discover facts, and I tell you what facts I discover with these methods. I cannot discover a castration complex or a repressed incest or something like that – I find only psychological facts, not theories. I am afraid you mix up too much theory with fact and you are perhaps disappointed that the experiments do not reveal a castration complex and such things, but a castration complex is a theory. What you find in the association method are definite facts which we did not know before and which the test person also did not know in this particular light. I do not say he did not know it under another light. You know many things when you are in your business that you do not know at home, and at home you know many things that you do not know in your official position. Things are known in one place and somewhere else they are not known. That is what we call unconscious. I must repeat that we cannot penetrate the unconscious empirically and then discover, for instance, the Freudian theory of the castration complex. The castration complex is a mythological idea, but it is not found as such. What we actually find are certain facts grouped in a specific way, and we name them according to mythological or historical parallels. You cannot find a mythological motif, you can only find a personal motif, and that never appears in the form of a theory but as a living fact of human life. You can abstract a theory from it, Freudian or Adlerian or any other. You can think what you please about the facts of the world, and there will be as many theories in the end as heads that think about it.

Dr Suttie:

I protest! I am not interested in this or that theory or what facts are found or not, but I am interested in having a means of communication by which each can know what the others are thinking and for that end I hold that our conceptions must be defined. We must know what the other person means by a certain thing like the unconscious of Freud. As for the word 'unconscious', it is becoming more or less known to everybody. It has therefore a certain social or illustrative value, but Jung refuses to recognize the word 'unconscious' in the meaning Freud gives to it and uses 'unconscious' in a way that we have come to consider as what Freud calls the 'Id'.

Professor Jung:

The word 'unconscious' is not Freud's invention. It was known in German philosophy long before, by Kant and Leibniz and others, and each of them gives his definition of that term. I am perfectly well aware that there are many different conceptions of the unconscious, and what I was trying humbly to do was to say what I think about it. It is not that I undervalue the merits of Leibniz, Kant, von Hartmann, or any other great man, including Freud and Adler and so on. I was only explaining what I mean by the unconscious, and I presuppose that you are all aware of what Freud means by it. I did not think it was my task to explain things in such a way that somebody who is convinced of Freud's theory and prefers that point of view would be upset in his belief. I have no tendency to destroy your convictions or points of view. I simply exhibit my own point of view, and if anybody should be tempted to think that this also is reasonable, that is all I want. It is perfectly indifferent to me what one thinks about the unconscious in general, otherwise I should begin a long dissertation on the concept of the unconscious as understood by Leibniz, Kant, and von Hartmann.

Dr Suttie:

Dr Strauss asked about the relationship of the unconscious as conceived by you and by Freud. Is it possible to bring them into precise and definite relationship?

Professor Jung:

Dr Graham Howe has answered the question. Freud is seeing the mental processes as static, while I speak in terms of dynamics and relationship. To me all is relative. There is nothing definitely unconscious; it is only not present to the conscious mind under a certain light. You can have very different ideas of why a thing is known under one aspect and not known under another aspect. The only exception I make is the mythological pattern, which is profoundly unconscious, as I can prove by the facts.

Dr Strauss:

Surely there is a difference between using your association test as a crime detector and for finding, let us say, unconscious guilt. Your criminal is conscious of his guilt and he is conscious that he is afraid of its being discovered. Your neurotic is unaware of his guilt and unaware that he is afraid of his guilt. Can the same kind of technique be used in these two very different kinds of cases?

The Chairman:

This woman was not conscious of her guilt though she had allowed the child to suck the sponge.

Professor Jung:

I will show you the difference experimentally. In Figure 7 you have a short illustration of respiration during the association test. You see four series of seven respirations registered after the stimulus words. The diagrams are condensations of respirations after indifferent and critical stimulus words in a greater number of test persons.

'A' gives respirations after indifferent stimulus words. The first inspirations after the stimulus words are restricted, while the following inspirations are of normal size.

In 'B' where the stimulus word was a critical one the volume of breathing is definitely restricted, sometimes by more than half the normal size.

In 'C' we have the behaviour of breathing after a stimulus word relating to a complex that was conscious to the test persons. The first inspiration is almost normal, and only later you find a certain restriction.

In 'D' the respiration is after a stimulus word that was related to a complex of which the test persons were unconscious. In this case the first inspiration is remarkably small and the following are rather below normal.

These diagrams illustrate very clearly the difference of reaction between conscious and unconscious complexes. In 'C', for instance, the complex is conscious. The stimulus word hits the test person, and there is a deep inspiration. But when the stimulus word hits an unconscious complex, the volume of breathing is restricted, as shown in 'D' I. There is a spasm in the thorax, so that almost no breathing takes place. In that way one has empirical proof of the physiological difference between conscious and unconscious reaction.[14]

Dr Wilfred R. Bion:

You gave an analogy between archaic forms of the body and archaic forms of the mind. Is it purely an analogy or is there in fact a closer relationship?

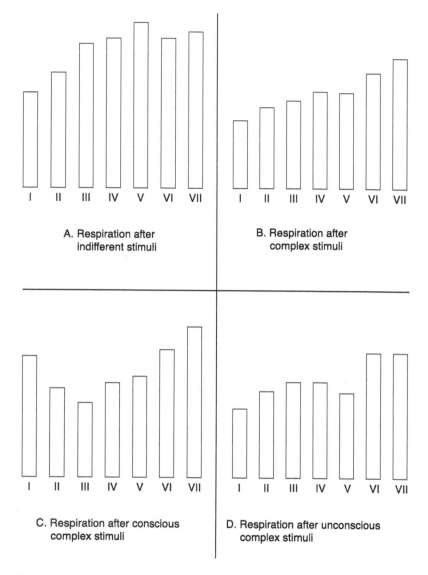

Figure 7 Association Test: Respiration

Last night you said something which suggested that you consider there is a connection between the mind and the brain, and there has lately been published in the *British Medical Journal* a diagnosis of yours from a dream of a physical disorder.[15] If that case was correctly reported it makes a very important suggestion, and I wondered whether you considered there was some closer connection between the two forms of archaic survival.

Professor Jung:

You touch again on the controversial problem of psychophysical parallelism for which I know of no answer, because it is beyond the reach of man's cognition. As I tried to explain yesterday, the two things – the psychic fact and the physiological fact – come together in a peculiar way. They happen together and are, so I assume, simply two different aspects to our mind, but not in reality. We see them as two on account of the utter incapacity of our mind to think them together. Because of that possible unity of the two things, we must expect to find dreams which are more on the physiological side than on the psychological, as we have other dreams that are more on the psychological than on the physical side. The dream to which you refer was very clearly a representation of an organic disorder. These 'organic representations' are well known in ancient literature. The doctors of antiquity and of the Middle Ages used dreams for their diagnosis. I did not conduct a physical examination on the man you refer to. I only heard his history and was told the dream, and I gave my opinion on it. I have had other cases, for instance a very doubtful case of progressive muscular atrophy in a young girl. I asked about dreams and she had two dreams which were very colourful. A colleague, a man who knew something of psychology, thought it might be a case of hysteria. There were indeed hysterical symptoms, and it was still doubtful if it was progressive muscular atrophy or not; but on account of the dreams I came to the conclusion that it must be an organic disease, and the end proved my diagnosis. It was an organic disturbance, and the dreams were definitely referring to the organic condition.[16] According to my idea of the community of the psyche and the living body it should be like that, and it would be marvellous if it were not so.

Dr Bion:

Will you be talking of that later when you speak on dreams?

Professor Jung:

I am afraid that I cannot go into such detail; it is too special. It is really a matter of special experience, and its presentation would be a very difficult job. It would not be possible to describe to you briefly the criteria by which I judge such dreams. The dream you mentioned, you may remember, was a dream of the little mastodon. To explain what that mastodon really means in an organic respect and why I must take that dream as an organic symptom would start such an argument that you would accuse me of the most terrible obscurantism. These things really are obscure. I had to speak in terms of the basic mind, which thinks in archetypal patterns. When I speak of archetypal patterns those who are aware of these things understand, but if you are not aware you think, 'This fellow is absolutely crazy because he talks of mastodons and their difference from snakes and horses'. I should have to give you a course of about four semesters about symbology first so that you could appreciate what I said.

That is the great trouble: there is such a gap between what is usually known of these things and what I have worked on all these years. If I were to speak of this even before a medical audience I should have to talk of the peculiarities of the *niveau mental*, to quote Janet, and I might as well talk Chinese. For instance, I would say that the *abaissement du niveau mental* sank in a certain case to the level of the *manipura chakra*,[17] that is to the level of the navel. We Europeans are not the only people on the earth. We are just a peninsula of Asia, and on that continent there are old civilizations where people have trained their minds in introspective psychology for thousands of years, whereas we began with our psychology not even yesterday but only this morning. These people have an insight that is simply fabulous, and I had to study Eastern things to understand certain facts of the unconscious. I had to go back to understand Oriental symbolism. I am about to publish a little book on one symbolic motif only,[18] and you will find it hair-raising. I had to study not only Chinese and Hindu but Sanskrit literature and medieval Latin manuscripts which are not even known to specialists, so that one must go to the British Museum to find the references. Only when you possess that apparatus of parallelism can you begin to make diagnoses and say that this dream is organic and that one is not. Until people have acquired that knowledge I am just a sorcerer. They say it is *un tour de passe-passe*. They said it in the Middle Ages. They said, 'How can you see that Jupiter has satellites?' If you reply that you have a telescope, what is a telescope to a medieval audience?

I do not mean to boast about this. I am always perplexed when my colleagues ask: 'How do you establish such a diagnosis or come to this conclusion?' I reply: 'I will explain if you will allow me to explain what you ought to know to be able to understand it'. I experienced this myself when the famous Einstein was Professor at Zurich. I often saw him, and it was when he was beginning to work on his theory of relativity. He was often in my house, and I pumped him about his relativity theory. I am not gifted in mathematics and you should have seen all the trouble the poor man had to explain relativity to me. He did not know how to do it. I went fourteen feet deep into the floor and felt quite small when I saw how he was troubled. But one day he asked me something about psychology. Then I had my revenge.

Special knowledge is a terrible disadvantage. It leads you in a way too far, so that you cannot explain any more. You must allow me to talk to you about seemingly elementary things, but if you will accept them I think you will understand why I draw such and such conclusions. I am sorry that we do not have more time and that I cannot tell you everything. When I come to dreams I have to give myself away and to risk your thinking me a perfect fool, because I am not able to put before you all the historical evidence which led to my conclusions. I should have to quote bit after bit from Chinese and Hindu literature, medieval texts and all the things which you do not know. How could you? I am working with specialists in other fields of knowledge and they help me. There was my late friend Professor Wilhelm, the sinologist; I worked with him. He had translated a Taoist text, and he asked me to comment on it, which I did from the psychological side.[19] I am a terrible novelty to a sinologist, but what he has to tell us is a novelty to us. The Chinese philosophers were no fools. We think the old people were fools, but they were as intelligent as we are. They were frightfully intelligent people, and psychology can learn no end from old civilizations, particularly from India and China. A former President of the British Anthropological Society asked me: 'Can you understand that such a highly intelligent people as the Chinese have no science?' I replied: 'They have a science, but you do not understand it. It is not based on the principle of causality. The principle of causality is not the only principle; it is only relative'.

People may say: What a fool to say causality is only relative! But look at modern physics! The East bases its thinking and its evaluation of facts on another principle. We have not even a word for that principle. The East naturally has a word for it, but we do not understand it. The Eastern word is Tao. My friend McDougall[20] has a Chinese student, and he asked him: 'What exactly do you mean by Tao?' Typically Western! The Chinese explained what Tao is and he replied: 'I do not understand yet'. The Chinese went out to the balcony and said: 'What do you see?' 'I see a street and houses and people walking and tram-cars passing'. 'What more?' 'There is a hill'. 'What more?' 'Trees'. 'What more?' 'The wind is blowing'. The Chinese threw up his arms and said: 'That is Tao'.

There you are. Tao can be anything. I use another word to designate it, but it is poor enough. I call it synchronicity. The Eastern mind, when it looks at an ensemble of facts, accepts that ensemble as it is, but the Western mind divides it into entities, small quantities. You look, for instance, at this present gathering of people, and you say: 'Where do they come from? Why should they come together?' The Eastern mind is not at all interested in that. It says: 'What does it mean that these people are together?' That is not a problem for the Western mind. You are interested in what you come here for and what you are doing here. Not so the Eastern mind; it is interested in being together.

It is like this: you are standing on the sea-shore and the waves wash up an old hat, an old box, a shoe, a dead fish, and there they lie on the shore. You say: 'Chance, nonsense!' The Chinese mind asks: 'What does it mean that these things are together?' The Chinese mind experiments with that *being together and coming together at the right moment*, and it has an experimental method which is not known in the West, but which plays a large role in the philosophy of the East. It is a method of forecasting possibilities, and it is still used by the Japanese Government about political situations; it was used, for instance, in the Great War. This method was formulated in 1143 B.C.[21]

NOTES

1   [Cf. *The Archetypes and the Collective Unconscious* (C.W., vol. 9, i), par. 5.]
2   See *Psychology of the Unconscious* [or *Symbols of Transformation* (C.W., vol. 5), index, s.v.].
3   [Henri Hubert and Marcel Mauss, *Mélanges d'histoire des religions*, p.xxix.]
4   [Cf. *Symbols of Transformation*, par. 154.]
5   [Cf. 'Psychology and Literature' (C.W., vol. 15), par. 150; 'Psychology and Religion' (C.W., vol. 11), par. 100, and 'Brother Klaus' (ibid.), par. 484. Documentation of the Rhodesian 'sun-wheels' has not been possible, though such rock-carved forms are noted in Angola and South Africa: cf. Willcox, *The Rock Art of South Africa*, fig. 23 and pls. xvii–xx. Their dating is in doubt. The 'rhino with tick-birds' is from the Transvaal and is in a museum in Pretoria. It was discovered in 1928 and widely publicized.]
6   [Albrecht Dieterich, *Eine Mithrasliturgie*.]
7   [*Symbols of Transformation*, pars. 151ff.; *The Archetypes and the Collective Unconscious*, par. 105; *The Structure and Dynamics of the Psyche* (C.W., vol. 8), pars. 228 and 318f.]
8   *How Natives Think*, trans. by Lilian A. Clare.
9   For general description of types and functions, see *Psychological Types*, Chap. X.
10 [Cf. Terence, *Heauton Timorumenos*, 1.1.25: 'Homo sum; humani nil a me alienum puto' (I am a man; I count nothing human alien to me).]
11 [*Civilization in Transition* (C.W., vol. 10), pars. 94ff. and 946ff.]
12 *Studies in Word Association*, tr. Eder. [Also in *Experimental Researches* (C.W., vol. 2).]
13 *Two Essays on Analytical Psychology* (C.W., vol. 7), pars. 245f., 304f.
14 [Cf. supra, p. 28, n. 15.]
15 [Cf. T. M. Davie, 'Comments upon a Case of "Periventricular Epilepsy" ', *British Medical Journal*, no. 3893 (Aug. 17, 1935), 293–297. The dream is reported by a patient of Davie as follows: 'Someone beside me kept on asking me something about oiling some machinery. Milk was suggested as the best lubricant. Apparently I thought that oozy slime was preferable. Then a pond was drained, and amid the slime there were two extinct animals. One was a minute mastodon. I forgot what the other one was'.
    Davie's comment: 'I thought it would be of interest to submit this dream to Jung to ask what his interpretation would be. He had no hesitation in saying that it indicated some organic disturbance, and that the illness was not primarily a psychological one, although there were numerous psychological derivatives in the dream. The drainage of the pond he interpreted as the damming-up of the cerebrospinal fluid circulation'.]
16 [*The Practice of Psychotherapy* (C.W., vol. 16), pars. 344f.]
17 [Cf. supra, p. 27, n. 4.]

18   [The mandala motif, in a lecture, 'Traumsymbole des Individuations-prozesses', that Jung delivered a few weeks previously at the Eranos Tagung. It was published the next year in *Eranos-Jahrbuch 1935*; in translation, as 'Dream Symbols of the Process of Individuation', *The Integration of the Personality*, 1939; revised as Part II of *Psychologie und Alchemie*, 1944 (= C.W., vol. 12). See also infra, p. 144.]

19   *The Secret of the Golden Flower*. [The Chinese text was translated by Richard Wilhelm. The commentary by Jung is contained in *Alchemical Studies* (C.W., vol. 13).]

20   [William McDougall (1871–1938), American psychiatrist. Cf. Jung's 'On the Psychogenesis of Schizophrenia' (C.W., vol. 3), par. 504, and 'The Therapeutic Value of Abreaction' (C.W., vol. 16), par. 255.]

21   [Cf. *The I Ching, or Book of Changes*, tr. Wilhelm/Baynes, 3rd edn., introduction, p. liii.]

LECTURE THREE

The Chairman (Dr Maurice B.Wright):

Ladies and Gentlemen, it is my privilege to be the Chairman at Professor Jung's lecture at this evening's meeting. It was my privilege twenty-one years ago to meet Professor Jung when he came over to London to give a series of addresses,[1] but there was then a very small group of psychologically minded physicians. I remember very well how after the meetings we used to go to a little restaurant in Soho and talk until we were turned out. Naturally we were trying to pump Professor Jung as hard as we could. When I said goodbye to Professor Jung he said to me – he did not say it very seriously – 'I think you are an extrovert who has become an introvert'. Frankly, I have been brooding about that ever since!

Now, ladies and gentlemen, just a word about last night. I think Professor Jung gave us a very good illustration of his views and of his work when he talked about the value of the telescope. A man with a telescope naturally can see a good deal more than anybody with unaided sight. That is exactly Professor Jung's position. With his particular spectacles, with his very specialized research, he has acquired a knowledge, a vision of the depth of the human psyche, which for many of us is very difficult to grasp. Of course, it will be impossible for him in the space of a few lectures to give us more than a very short outline of the vision he has gained. Therefore, in my opinion anything which might seem blurred or dark is not a question of obscurantism, it is a question of spectacles. My own difficulty is that, with my muscles of accommodation already hardening, it might be impossible for me ever to see that vision clearly, even if for the moment Professor Jung could lend me his spectacles. But however this may be, I know that we are all thrilled with everything he can tell us, and we know how stimulating it is to our own thinking, especially in a domain where speculation is so easy and where proof is so difficult.

Professor Jung:

Ladies and Gentlemen, I ought to have finished my lecture on the association tests yesterday, but I would have had to overstep my time. So you must pardon me for coming back to the same thing once more. It is not that I am particularly in love with the association tests. I use them only when I must, but they are really the foundation of certain conceptions. I told you last time about the characteristic disturbances, and I think it would be a good thing, perhaps, if I were briefly to sum up all there is to say about the results of the experiment, namely about the complexes.

A complex is an agglomeration of associations — a sort of picture of a more or less complicated psychological nature — sometimes of traumatic character, sometimes simply of a painful and highly toned character. Everything that is highly toned is rather difficult to handle. If, for instance, something is very important to me, I begin to hesitate when I attempt to do it, and you have probably observed that when you ask me difficult questions I cannot answer them immediately because the subject is important and I have a long reaction time. I begin to stammer, and my memory does not supply the necessary material. Such disturbances are complex disturbances — even if what I say does not come from a personal complex of mine. It is simply an important affair, and whatever has an intense feeling-tone is difficult to handle because such contents are somehow associated with physiological reactions, with the processes of the heart, the tonus of the blood vessels, the condition of the intestines, the breathing, and the innervation of the skin. Whenever there is a high tonus it is just as if that particular complex had a body of its own, as if it were localized in my body to a certain extent, and that makes it unwieldy, because something that irritates my body cannot be easily pushed away because it has its roots in my body and begins to pull at my nerves. Something that has little tonus and little emotional value can be easily brushed aside because it has no roots. It is not adherent or adhesive.

Ladies and Gentlemen, that leads me to something very important — the fact that a complex with its given tension or energy has the tendency to form a little personality of itself. It has a sort of body, a certain amount of its own physiology. It can upset the stomach. It upsets the breathing, it disturbs the heart — in short, it behaves like a partial personality. For instance, when you want to say or do something and unfortunately a complex interferes with this intention, then you say or do something different from what you intended. You are simply interrupted, and your best intention gets upset by the complex, exactly as if you had been interfered with by a human being or by circumstances from outside. Under those conditions we really are forced to speak of the tendencies of complexes to act as if they were characterized by a certain amount of will-power. When you speak of will-power you naturally ask about the ego. Where then is the ego that belongs to the will-power of the complexes? We know our own ego-complex, which is supposed to be in full possession of the body. It is not, but let us assume that it is a centre in full possession of the body, that there is a focus which we call the ego, and that the ego has a will and can do something with its components. The ego also is an agglomeration of highly toned contents, so that in principle there is no difference between the ego-complex and any other complex.

Because complexes have a certain will-power, a sort of ego, we find that in a schizophrenic condition they emancipate themselves from conscious control to such an extent that they become visible and audible. They appear as visions, they speak in voices which are like the voices of definite people. This personification of complexes is not in itself necessarily a pathological condition. In dreams, for instance, our complexes often appear in a personified form. And one can train oneself to such an extent that they become visible or audible also in a waking condition. It is part of a certain yoga training to split up consciousness into its components, each of which appears as a specific personality. In the psychology of our unconscious there are typical figures that have a definite life of their own.[2]

All this is explained by the fact that the so-called unity of consciousness is an illusion. It is really a wish-dream. We like to think that we are one; but we are not, most decidedly not. We are not really masters in our house. We like to believe in our will-power and in our energy and in what we can do; but when it comes to a real show-down we find that we can do it only to a certain extent, because we are hampered by those little devils the complexes. Complexes are autonomous groups of associations that have a tendency to move by themselves, to live their own life apart from our intentions. I hold that our personal unconscious, as well as the collective unconscious, consists of an indefinite, because unknown, number of complexes or fragmentary personalities.

This idea explains a lot. It explains, for instance, the simple fact that a poet has the capacity to dramatize and personify his mental contents. When he creates a character on the stage, or in his poem or drama or novel, he thinks it is merely a product of his imagination; but that character in a certain secret way has made itself. Any novelist or writer will deny that these characters have a psychological meaning, but as a matter of fact you know as well as I do that they have one. Therefore you can read a writer's mind when you study the characters he creates.

The complexes, then, are partial or fragmentary personalities. When we speak of the ego-complex, we naturally assume that it has a consciousness, because the relationship of the various contents to the centre, in other words to the ego, is called consciousness. But we also have a grouping of contents about a centre, a sort of nucleus, in other complexes. So we may ask the question: Do complexes have a consciousness of their own? If you study spiritualism, you must admit that the so-called spirits manifested in automatic writing or through the voice of a medium do indeed have a sort of consciousness of their own. Therefore unprejudiced people are inclined to believe that the spirits are the ghosts of a deceased aunt or grandfather or something of the kind, just on account of the more or less distinct personality which can be traced in these manifestations. Of course, when we are dealing with a case of insanity we are less inclined to assume that we have to do with ghosts. We call it pathological then.

So much about the complexes. I insist on that particular point of consciousness within complexes only because complexes play a large role in dream-analysis. You remember my diagram (Figure 4) showing the different spheres of the mind and the dark centre of the unconscious in the middle. The closer you approach that centre, the more you experience what Janet calls an *abaissement du niveau mental*: your conscious autonomy begins to disappear, and you get more and more under the fascination of unconscious contents. Conscious autonomy loses its tension and its energy, and that energy reappears in the increased activity of unconscious contents. You can observe this process in an extreme form when you carefully study a case of insanity. The fascination of unconscious contents gradually grows stronger and conscious control vanishes in proportion until finally the patient sinks into the unconscious altogether and becomes completely victimized by it. He is the victim of a new autonomous activity that does not start from his ego but starts from the dark sphere.

In order to deal with the association test thoroughly, I must mention an entirely different experiment. You will forgive me if for the sake of economizing time I do not go into the details of the researches, but these diagrams (Figs. 8, 9, 10, 11) illustrate the results of very voluminous researches into families.[3] They represent the quality of associations. For instance, the little summit in Figure 8 designated as number XI is a special class or category of association. The principle of classification is logical and linguistic. I am not going into this, and you will simply have to accept the fact that I have made fifteen categories into which I divide associations. We made tests with a great number of families, all for certain reasons uneducated people, and we found that the type of association and reaction is peculiarly parallel among certain members of the family; for instance, father and mother, or two brothers, or mother and child are almost identical in their type of reaction.

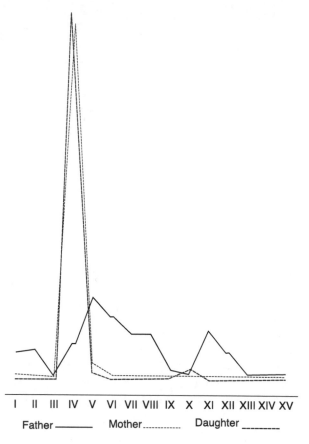

I   II   III   IV   V   VI   VII   VIII   IX   X   XI   XII   XIII XIV XV

Father ———   Mother ....   Daughter _____

Figure 8 Association Test of a Family

This was a very unfortunate marriage. The father was an alcoholic and the mother was a very peculiar type. You see that the sixteen-year-old daughter follows her mother's type closely. As much as thirty per cent of all associations are identical words. This is a striking case of participation, of mental contagion. If you think about this case you can draw certain conclusions. The mother was forty-five years old, married to an alcoholic. Her life was therefore a failure. Now the daughter has exactly the same reactions as the mother. If such a girl comes out into the world as though she were forty-five years old and married to an alcoholic, think what a mess she will get into! This participation explains why the daughter of an alcoholic who has had a hell of a youth will seek a man who is an alcoholic and marry him; and if by chance

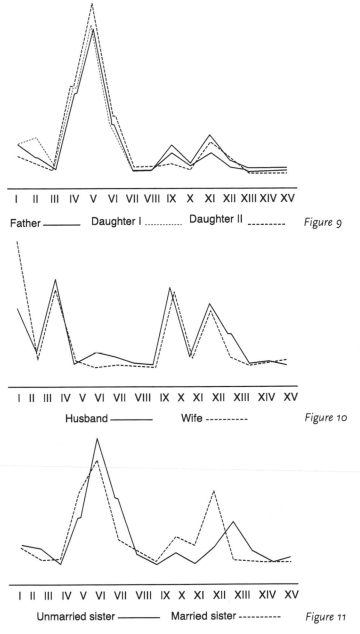

I   II   III   IV   V   VI   VII   VIII   IX   X   XI   XII   XIII   XIV   XV

Father ——— Daughter I .... Daughter II _____   *Figure 9*

I   II   III   IV   V   VI   VII   VIII   IX   X   XI   XII   XIII   XIV   XV

Husband ——— Wife ----------   *Figure 10*

I   II   III   IV   V   VI   VII   VIII   IX   X   XI   XII   XIII   XIV   XV

Unmarried sister ——— Married sister ----------   *Figure 11*

Figures 9–11 Association Tests of Families

he should not be one, she will make him into one on account of that peculiar identity with one member of the family.

Figure 9 is a very striking case, too. The father, who was a widower, had two daughters who lived with him in complete identity. Of course, that also is most unnatural, because either he reacts like a girl or the two girls react like a man, even in the way they speak. The whole mental make-up is poisoned through the admixture of an alien element, because a young daughter is not in actual fact her father.

Figure 10 is the case of a husband and wife. This diagram gives an optimistic tone to my very pessimistic demonstrations. You see there is perfect harmony here; but do not make the mistake of thinking that this harmony is a paradise, for these people will kick against each other after a while because they are just too harmonious. A very good harmony in a family based on participation soon leads to frantic attempts on the part of the spouses to kick loose from each other, to liberate themselves, and then they invent irritating topics of discussion in order to have a reason for feeling misunderstood. If you study the ordinary psychology of marriage, you discover that most of the troubles consist in this cunning invention of irritating topics which have absolutely no foundation.

Figure 11 is also interesting. These two women are sisters living together; one is single and the other married. Their summit is found at number V. The wife in Figure 10 is the sister of these two women in Figure 11, and while most probably they were all of the same type originally, she married a man of another type. Their summit is at number III in Figure 10. The condition of identity or participation which is demonstrated in the association test can be substantiated by entirely different experiences, for instance, by graphology. The handwriting of many wives, particularly young wives, often resembles that of the husband. I do not know whether it is so in these days, but I assume that human nature remains very much the same. Occasionally it is the other way round because the so-called feeble sex has its strength sometimes.

Ladies and Gentlemen, we are now going to step over the border into dreams. I do not want to give you any particular introduction to dream-analysis.[4] I think the best way is just to show you how I proceed with a dream, and then it does not need much explanation of a theoretical kind, because you can see what are my underlying ideas. Of course, I make great use of dreams, because dreams are an objective source of information in psychotherapeutic treatment. When a doctor has a case, he can hardly refrain from having ideas about it. But the more one knows about cases, the more one should make an heroic effort not to know in order to give the patient a fair chance. I always try not to know and not to see. It is much better to say you are stupid, or play what is apparently a stupid role, in order to give the patient a chance to come out with his own material. That does not mean that you should hide altogether.

This is a case of a man forty years old, a married man who has not been ill before. He looks quite all right; he is the director of a great public school, a very intelligent fellow who has studied an old-fashioned kind of psychology, Wundt psychology,[5] that has nothing to do with details of human life but moves in the stratosphere of abstract ideas. Recently he had been badly troubled by neurotic symptoms. He suffered from a peculiar kind of vertigo that seized upon him from time to time, palpitation, nausea, and peculiar attacks of feebleness and a sort of exhaustion. This syndrome presents the picture of a sickness which is well known in Switzerland. It is mountain sickness, a malady to which people who are not used to great heights are easily subject when climbing. So I asked, 'Is it not mountain sickness you are suffering from?' He said, 'Yes, you are right. It feels exactly like mountain sickness'. I asked him if he had dreams and he said that recently he had had three dreams.

I do not like to analyse one dream alone, because a single dream can be interpreted arbitrarily. You can speculate anything about an isolated dream; but if you compare a series of, say, twenty or a hundred dreams, then you can see interesting things. You see the process that is going on in the unconscious from night to night, and the continuity of the unconscious psyche extending through day and night. Presumably we are dreaming all the time, although we are not aware of it by day because consciousness is much too clear. But at night, when there is that *abaissement du niveau mental*, the dreams can break through and become visible.

In the first dream *the patient finds himself in a small village in Switzerland. He is a very solemn black figure in a long coat; under his arm he carries several thick books. There is a group of young boys whom he recognizes as having been his classmates. They are looking at him and they say: 'That fellow does not often make his appearance here'.*

In order to understand this dream you have to remember that the patient is in a very fine position and has had a very good scientific education. But he started really from the bottom and is a self-made man. His parents were very poor peasants, and he worked his way up to his present position. He is very ambitious and is filled with the hope that he will rise still higher. He is like a man who has climbed in one day from sea-level to a level of 6,000 feet, and there he sees peaks 12,000 feet high towering above him. He finds himself in the place from which one climbs these higher mountains, and because of this he forgets all about the fact that he has already climbed 6,000 feet and immediately he starts to attack the higher peaks. But as a matter of fact though he does not realize it he is tired from his climbing and quite incapable of going any further at this time. This lack of realization is the reason for his symptoms of mountain sickness. The dream brings home to him the actual psychological situation. The contrast of himself as the solemn figure in the long black coat with thick books under his arm appearing in his native village, and of the village boys remarking that he does not often appear there, means that he does not often remember where he came from. On the contrary he thinks of his future career and hopes to get a chair as professor. Therefore the dream puts him back into his early surroundings. He ought to realize how much he has achieved considering who he was originally and that there are natural limitations to human effort.

The beginning of the second dream is a typical instance of the kind of dream that occurs when the conscious attitude is like his. *He knows that he ought to go to an important conference, and he is taking his portfolio. But he notices that the hour is rather advanced and that the train will leave soon, and so he gets into that well-known state of haste and of fear of being too late. He tries to get his clothes together, his hat is nowhere, his coat is mislaid, and he runs about in search of them and shouts up and down the house, 'Where are my things?' Finally he gets everything together, and runs out of the house only to find that he has forgotten his portfolio. He rushes back for it, and looking at his watch finds how late it is getting; then he runs to the station, but the road is quite soft so that it is like walking on a bog and his feet can hardly move any more. Pantingly he arrives at the station only to see that the train is just leaving. His attention is called to the railway track, and it looks like this:*

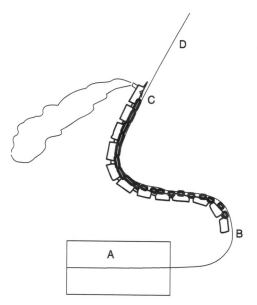

Figure 12 Dream of the Train

He is at A, the tail-end of the train is already at B and the engine is at C. He watches the train, a long one, winding round the curve, and he thinks, 'If only the engine-driver, when he reaches point

D, has sufficient intelligence not to rush full steam ahead; for if he does, the long train behind him which will still be rounding the curve will be derailed'. Now the engine-driver arrives at D and he opens the steam throttle fully, the engine begins to pull, and the train rushes ahead. The dreamer sees the catastrophe coming, the train goes off the rails, and he shouts, and then he wakes up with the fear characteristic of nightmare.

Whenever one has this kind of dream of being late, of a hundred obstacles interfering, it is exactly the same as when one is in such a situation in reality, when one is nervous about something. One is nervous because there is an unconscious resistance to the conscious intention. The most irritating thing is that consciously you want something very much, and an unseen devil is always working against it, and of course you are that devil too. You are working against this devil and do it in a nervous way and with nervous haste. In the case of this dreamer, that rushing ahead is also against his will. He does not want to leave home, yet he wants it very much, and all the resistance and difficulties in his way are his own doing. He is that engine-driver who thinks, 'Now we are out of our trouble; we have a straight line ahead, and now we can rush along like anything'. The straight line beyond the curve would correspond to the peaks 12,000 feet high, and he thinks these peaks are accessible to him.

Naturally, nobody seeing such a chance ahead would refrain from making the utmost use of it, so his reason says to him, 'Why not go on, you have every chance in the world'. He does not see why something in him should work against it. But this dream gives him a warning that he should not be as stupid as this engine-driver who goes full steam ahead when the tail-end of the train is not yet out of the curve. That is what we always forget; we always forget that our consciousness is only a surface, our consciousness is the avant-garde of our psychological existence. Our head is only one end, but behind our consciousness is a long historical 'tail' of hesitations and weaknesses and complexes and prejudices and inheritances, and we always make our reckoning without them. We always think we can make a straight line in spite of our shortcomings, but they will weigh very heavily and often we derail before we have reached our goal because we have neglected our tail-ends.

I always say that our psychology has a long saurian's tail behind it, namely the whole history of our family, of our nation, of Europe, and of the world in general. We are always human, and we should never forget that we carry the whole burden of being only human. If we were heads only we should be like little angels that have heads and wings, and of course they can do what they please because they are not hindered by a body that can walk only on the earth. I must not omit to point out, not necessarily to the patient but to myself, that this peculiar movement of the train is like a snake. Presently we shall see why.

The next dream is the crucial dream, and I shall have to give certain explanations. In this dream we have to do with a peculiar animal which is half lizard and half crab. Before we go into the details of the dream, I want to make a few remarks about the method of working out the meaning of a dream. You know that there are many views and many misunderstandings as to the way in which you get at dreams.

You know, for instance, what is understood by free association. This method is a very doubtful one as far as my experience goes. Free association means that you open yourself to any amount and kind of associations and they naturally lead to your complexes. But then, you see, I do not want to know the complexes of my patients. That is uninteresting to me. I want to know what the dreams have to say about complexes, not what the complexes are. I want to know what a man's unconscious is doing with his complexes, I want to know what he is preparing himself for. That is what I read out of the dreams. If I wanted to apply the method of free association I would not need dreams. I could put up a signboard, for instance 'Footpath to So-and-so', and simply let people meditate on that and add free associations, and they would invariably arrive at their complexes. If you are riding in a Hungarian or Russian train and look at the strange signs in the strange language, you can associate all your complexes. You have only to let yourself go and you naturally drift into your complexes.

I do not apply the method of free association because my goal is not to know the complexes; I want to know what the dream is. Therefore I handle the dream as if it were a text which I do not understand properly, say a Latin or a Greek or a Sanskrit text, where certain words are unknown to me or the text is fragmentary, and I merely apply the ordinary method any philologist would apply in reading such a text. My idea is that the dream does not conceal; we simply do not understand its language. For instance, if I quote to you a Latin or a Greek passage some of you will not understand it, but that is not because the text dissimulates or conceals; it is because you do not know Greek or Latin. Likewise, when a patient seems confused, it does not necessarily mean that he is confused, but that the doctor does not understand his material. The assumption that the dream wants to conceal is a mere anthropomorphic idea. No philologist would ever think that a difficult Sanskrit or cuneiform inscription conceals. There is a very wise word of the Talmud which says that the dream is its own interpretation. The dream is the whole thing, and if you think there is something behind it, or that the dream has concealed something, there is no question but that you simply do not understand it.

Therefore, first of all, when you handle a dream you say, 'I do not understand a word of that dream.' I always welcome that feeling of incompetence because then I know I shall put some good work into my attempt to understand the dream. What I do is this. I adopt the method of the philologist, which is far from being free association, and apply a logical principle which is called *amplification*. It is simply that of seeking the parallels. For instance, in the case of a very rare word which you have never come across before, you try to find parallel text passages, parallel applications perhaps, where that word also occurs, and then you try to put the formula you have established from the knowledge of other texts into the new text. If you make the new text a readable whole, you say, 'Now we can read it'. That is how we learned to read hieroglyphics and cuneiform inscriptions and that is how we can read dreams.

Now, how do I find the context? Here I simply follow the principle of the association experiment. Let us assume a man dreams about a simple sort of peasant's house. Now, do I know what a simple peasant's house conveys to that man's mind? Of course not; how could I? Do I know what a simple peasant's house means to him in general? Of course not. So I simply ask, 'How does that thing appear to you?' – in other words, what is your context, what is the mental tissue in which that term 'simple peasant's house' is embedded? He will tell you something quite astonishing. For instance, somebody says 'water'. Do I know what he means by 'water'? Not at all. When I put that test word or a similar word to somebody, he will say 'green'. Another one will say 'H₂O', which is something quite different. Another one will say 'quicksilver', or 'suicide'. In each case I know what tissue that word or image is embedded in. That is *amplification*. It is a well-known logical procedure which we apply here and which formulates exactly the technique of finding the context.

Of course, I ought to mention here the merit of Freud, who brought up the whole question of dreams and who has enabled us to approach the problem of dreams at all. You know his idea is that a dream is a distorted representation of a secret incompatible wish which does not agree with the conscious attitude and therefore is censored, that is, distorted, in order to become unrecognizable to the conscious and yet in a way to show itself and live. Freud logically says then: Let us redress that whole distortion; now be natural, give up your distorted tendencies and let your associations flow freely, then we will come to your natural facts, namely, your complexes. This is an entirely different point of view from mine. Freud is seeking the complexes, I am not. That is just the difference. I am looking for what the *unconscious is doing* with the complexes, because that interests me very much more than the fact that people have complexes. We all have complexes; it is a highly banal and uninteresting fact. Even the incest complex which you can find anywhere if you look for it is terribly banal and therefore uninteresting. It is only interesting to know what people do with their complexes; that is the practical question which matters. Freud applies the method of free association and makes use of an entirely different logical principle, a principle which in logic is called *reductio in primam figuram*, reduction to the first figure. The *reductio in primam figuram* is a so-called syllogism, a complicated sequence of logical conclusions, whose characteristic is that you start from a perfectly reasonable statement, and, through surreptitious assumptions and insinuations, you gradually change the reasonable nature of your first simple or prime figure until you reach a complete distortion which is utterly unreasonable. That complete distortion, in Freud's idea, characterizes the dream; the dream is a clever distortion that disguises the original figure, and you have only to undo the web in order to return to the first reasonable statement, which may be 'I wish to commit this or that; I have such and such an incompatible wish'. We start, for instance, with a perfectly reasonable assumption, such as 'No unreasonable being is free' – in other words, has free will. This is an example which is used in logic. It is a fairly reasonable statement. Now we come to the first fallacy, 'Therefore, no free being is unreasonable'. You cannot quite agree because there is already a trick. Then you continue, 'All human beings are free' – they all have free will. Now you triumphantly finish up, 'Therefore no human being is unreasonable'. That is complete nonsense.

Let us assume that the dream is such an utterly nonsensical statement. This is perfectly plausible because obviously the dream is something like a nonsensical statement; otherwise you could understand it. As a rule you cannot understand it; you hardly ever come across dreams which are clear from beginning to end. The ordinary dream seems absolute nonsense and therefore one depreciates it. Even primitives, who make a great fuss about dreams, say that ordinary dreams mean nothing. But there are 'big' dreams; medicine men and chiefs have big dreams, but ordinary men have no dreams. They talk exactly like people in Europe. Now you are confronted with that dream-nonsense, and you say, 'This nonsense must be an insinuating distortion or fallacy which derives from an originally reasonable statement'. You undo the whole thing and you apply the *reductio in primam figuram* and then you come to the initial undisturbed statement. So you see that the procedure of Freud's dream-interpretation is perfectly logical, if you assume that the statement of the dream is really nonsensical.

But do not forget when you make the statement that a thing is unreasonable that perhaps you do not understand because you are not God; on the contrary, you are a fallible human being with a very limited mind. When an insane patient tells me something, I may think: 'What that fellow is talking about is all nonsense'. As a matter of fact, if I am scientific, I say 'I do not understand', but if I am unscientific, I say 'That fellow is just crazy and I am intelligent'. This argumentation is the reason why men with somewhat unbalanced minds often like to become alienists. It is humanly understandable because it gives you a tremendous satisfaction, when you are not quite sure of yourself, to be able to say 'Oh, the others are much worse'.

But the question remains: Can we safely say that a dream is nonsense? Are we quite sure that we know? Are we sure that the dream is a distortion?

Are you absolutely certain when you discover something quite against your expectation that it is a mere distortion? Nature commits no errors. Right and wrong are human categories. The natural process is just what it is and nothing else – it is not nonsense and it is not unreasonable. We do not understand: that is the fact. Since I am not God and since I am a man of very limited intellectual capacities, I had better assume that I do not understand dreams. With that assumption I reject the prejudiced view that the dream is a distortion, and I say that if I do not understand a dream, it is my mind which is distorted, I am not taking the right view of it.

So I adopted the method which philologists apply to difficult texts, and I handle dreams in the same way. It is, of course, a bit more circumstantial and more difficult; but I can assure you that the results are far more interesting when you arrive at things that are human than when you apply a most dreadful monotonous interpretation. I hate to be bored. Above all we should avoid speculations and theories when we have to deal with such mysterious processes as dreams. We should never forget that for thousands of years very intelligent men of great knowledge and vast experience held very different views about them. It is only quite recently that we invented the theory that a dream is nothing. All other civilizations have had very different ideas about dreams.

Now I will tell you the big dream of my patient: 'I am in the country, in a simple peasant's house, with an elderly, motherly peasant woman. I talk to her about a great journey I am planning: I am going to walk from Switzerland to Leipzig. She is enormously impressed, at which I am very pleased. At this moment I look through the window at a meadow where there are peasants gathering hay. Then the scene changes. In the background appears a monstrously big crab-lizard. It moves first to the left and then to the right so that I find myself standing in the angle between them as if in an open pair of scissors. Then I have a little rod or a wand in my hand, and I lightly touch the monster's head with the rod and kill it. Then for a long time I stand there contemplating that monster.'

Before I go into such a dream I always try to establish a sequence, because this dream has a history before and will have a history afterwards. It is part of the psychic tissue that is continuous, for we have no reason to assume that there is no continuity in the psychological processes, just as we have no reason to think that there is any gap in the processes of nature. Nature is a continuum, and so our psyche is very probably a continuum. This dream is just one flash or one observation of psychic continuity that became visible for a moment. As a continuity it is connected with the preceding dreams. In the previous dream we have already seen that peculiar snake-like movement of the train. This comparison is merely a hypothesis, but I have to establish such connections.

After the train-dream the dreamer is back in the surroundings of his early childhood; he is with a motherly peasant woman – a slight allusion to the mother, as you notice. In the very first dream, he impresses the village boys by his magnificent appearance in the long coat of the Herr Professor. In this present dream too he impresses the harmless woman with his greatness and the greatness of his ambitious plan to walk to Leipzig – an allusion to his hope of getting a chair there. The monster crab-lizard is outside our empirical experience; it is obviously a creation of the unconscious. So much we can see without any particular effort.

Now we come to the actual context. I ask him, 'What are your associations to "simple peasant's house"?' and to my enormous astonishment, he says 'It is the lazar-house of St Jacob near Basel'. This house was a very old leprosery, and the building still exists. The place is also famous for a big battle fought there in 1444 by the Swiss against the troops of the Duke of Burgundy. His army tried to break into Switzerland but was beaten back by the avant-garde of the Swiss army, a body of 1,300 men who fought the Burgundian army consisting of 30,000 men at the lazar-house of St Jacob. The 1,300 Swiss fell to the very last man, but by their sacrifice they stopped the further advance of the enemy. The heroic death of these 1,300 men is a notable incident in Swiss history, and no Swiss is able to talk of it without patriotic feeling.

Whenever the dreamer brings such a piece of information, you have to put it into the context of the dream. In this case it means that the dreamer is in a leprosery. The lazar-house is called 'Siechenhaus', sick-house, in German, the 'sick' meaning the lepers. So he has, as it were, a revolting contagious disease; he is an outcast from human society, he is in the sick-house. And that sick-house is characterized, moreover, by that desperate fight which was a catastrophe for the 1,300 men and which was brought about by the fact that they did not obey orders. The avant-garde had strict instructions not to attack but to wait until the whole of the Swiss army had joined up with them. But as soon as they saw the enemy they could not hold back and, against the commands of their leaders, made a headlong rush and attacked, and of course they were all killed. Here again we come to the idea of this rushing ahead without establishing a connection with the bulk of the tail-end, and again the action is fatal. This gave me a rather uncanny feeling, and I thought, 'Now what is the fellow after, what danger is he coming to?' The danger is not just his ambition, or that he wishes to be with the mother and commit incest, or something of the kind. You remember, the engine-driver is a foolish fellow too; he runs ahead in spite of the fact that the tail-end of the train is not yet out of the curve; he does not wait for it, but rushes along without thinking of the whole. That means that the dreamer has the tendency to rush ahead, not thinking of his tail; he behaves as if he were his head only, just as the avant-garde behaved as if it were the whole army, forgetting that it had to wait; and because it did not wait, every man was killed. This attitude of the patient is the reason for his symptoms of mountain sickness. He went too high, he is not prepared for the altitude, he forgets where he started from.

You know perhaps the novel by Paul Bourget, L' Étape. Its motif is the problem that a man's low origin always clings to him, and therefore there are very definite limitations to his climbing the social ladder. That is what the dream tries to remind the patient of. That house and that elderly peasant woman bring him back to his childhood. It looks, then, as if the woman might refer to the mother. But one must be careful with assumptions. His answer to my question about the woman was 'That is my landlady'. His landlady is an elderly widow, uneducated and old-fashioned, living naturally in a milieu inferior to his. He is too high up, and he forgets that the next part of his invisible self is the family in himself. Because he is a very intellectual man, feeling is his inferior function. His feeling is not at all differentiated, and therefore it is still in the form of the landlady, and in trying to impose upon that landlady he tries to impose upon himself with his enormous plan to walk to Leipzig.

Now what does he say about the trip to Leipzig? He says, 'Oh, that is my ambition, I want to go far, I wish to get a Chair'. Here is the headlong rush, here is the foolish attempt, here is the mountain sickness; he wants to climb too high. This dream was before the war, and at that time to be a professor in Leipzig was something marvellous. His feeling was deeply repressed; therefore it does not have right values and is much too naïve. It is still the peasant woman; it is still identical with his own mother. There are many capable and intelligent men who have no differentiation of feeling, and therefore their feeling is still contaminated with the mother, is still in the mother, identical with the mother, and they have mothers' feelings; they have wonderful feelings for babies, for the interiors of houses and nice rooms and for a very orderly home. It sometimes happens that these individuals, when they have turned forty, discover a masculine feeling, and then there is trouble.

The feelings of a man are so to speak a woman's and appear as such in dreams. I designate this figure by the term *anima*, because she is the personification of the inferior functions which relate a man to the collective unconscious. The collective unconscious as a whole presents itself to a man in feminine form. To a woman it appears in masculine form, and then I call it the *animus*. I chose the term anima because it has always been used for that very same psychological fact. The anima as a personification of the collective unconscious occurs in dreams over and over again.[6] I have made long statistics about the anima figure in dreams. In this way one establishes these figures empirically.

When I ask my dreamer what he means when he says that the peasant woman is impressed by his plan, he answers, 'Oh, well, that refers to my boasting. I like to boast before an inferior person to show who I am; when I am talking to uneducated people I like to put myself very much in the foreground. Unfortunately I have always to live in an inferior milieu'. When a man resents the inferiority of his milieu and feels that he is too good for his surroundings, it is because the inferiority of the milieu in himself is projected into the outer milieu and therefore he begins to mind those things which he should mind in himself. When he says, 'I mind my inferior milieu', he ought to say, 'I mind the fact that my own inner milieu is below the mark'. He has no right values, he is inferior in his feeling-life. That is his problem.

At this moment he looks out of the window and sees the peasants gathering hay. That, of course, again is a vision of something he has done in the past. It brings back to him memories of similar pictures and situations; it was in summer and it was pretty hard work to get up early in the morning to turn the hay during the day and gather it in the evening. Of course, it is the simple honest work of such folk. He forgets that only the decent simple work gets him somewhere and not a big mouth. He also asserts, which I must mention, that in his present home he has a picture on the wall of peasants gathering hay, and he says, 'Oh, that is the origin of the picture in my dream'. It is as though he said, 'The dream is nothing but a picture on the wall, it has no importance, I will pay no attention to it'. At that moment the scene changes. When the scene changes you can always safely conclude that a representation of an unconscious thought has come to a climax, and it becomes impossible to continue that motif.

Now in the next part of the dream things are getting dark; the crab-lizard appears, apparently an enormous thing. I asked, 'What about the crab, how on earth do you come to that?' He said, 'That is a mythological monster which walks backwards. The crab walks backwards. I do not understand how I get to this thing – probably through some fairytale or something of that sort'. What he had mentioned before were all things which you could meet with in real life, things which do actually exist. But the crab is not a personal experience, it is an archetype. When an analyst has to deal with an archetype he may begin to think. In dealing with the personal unconscious you are not allowed to think too much and to add anything to the associations of the patient. Can you add something to the personality of somebody else? You are a personality yourself. The other individual has a life of his own and a mind of his own inasmuch as he is a person. But inasmuch as he is not a person, inasmuch as he is also myself, he has the same basic structure of mind, and there I can begin to think, I can associate for him. I can even provide him with the necessary context because he will have none, he does not know where that crab-lizard comes from and has no idea what it means, but I know and can provide the material for him.

I point out to him that the hero motif appears throughout the dreams. He has a hero fantasy about himself which comes to the surface in the last dream. He is the hero as the great man with the long coat and with the great plan; he is the hero who dies on the field of honour at St Jacob; he is going to show the world who he is; and he is quite obviously the hero who overcomes the monster. The hero motif is invariably accompanied by the dragon motif; the dragon and the hero who fights him are two figures of the same myth.

The dragon appears in his dream as the crab-lizard. This statement does not, of course, explain what the dragon represents as an image of his psychological situation. So the next associations are directed round the monster. When it moves first to the left and then to the right the dreamer has the feeling that he is standing in an angle which could shut on him like open scissors. That would be fatal. He has read Freud, and accordingly he interprets the situation as an incest wish, the monster being the mother, the angle of the open scissors the legs of the mother, and he himself, standing in between, being just born or just going back into the mother.

Strangely enough, in mythology, the dragon is the mother. You meet that motif all over the world, and the monster is called the mother dragon.[7] The mother dragon eats the child again, she sucks him in after having given birth to him. The 'terrible mother', as she is also called, is waiting with wide-open mouth on the Western Seas, and when a man approaches that mouth it closes on him and he is finished. That monstrous figure is the mother sarcophaga, the flesh-eater; it is, in another form, Matuta, the mother of the dead. It is the goddess of death.

But these parallels still do not explain why the dream chooses the particular image of the crab. I hold – and when I say I hold I have certain reasons for saying so – that representations of psychic facts in images like the snake or the lizard or the crab or the mastodon or analogous animals also represent organic facts. For instance, the serpent very often represents the cerebro-spinal system, especially the lower centres of the brain, and particularly the medulla oblongata and spinal cord. The crab, on the other hand, having a sympathetic system only, represents chiefly the sympathicus and para-sympathicus of the abdomen; it is an abdominal thing. So if you translate the text of the dream it would read: if you go on like this your cerebro-spinal system and your sympathetic system will come up against you and snap you up. That is in fact what is happening. The symptoms of his neurosis express the rebellion of the sympathetic functions and of the cerebro-spinal system against his conscious attitude.

The crab-lizard brings up the archetypal idea of the hero and the dragon as deadly enemies. But in certain myths you find the interesting fact that the hero is not connected with the dragon only by his fight. There are, on the contrary, indications that the hero is himself the dragon. In Scandinavian mythology the hero is recognized by the fact that he has snake's eyes. He has snake's eyes because he is a snake. There are many other myths and legends which contain the same idea. Cecrops, the founder of Athens, was a man above and a serpent below. The souls of heroes often appear after death in the form of serpents.

Now in our dream the monstrous crab-lizard moves first to the left, and I ask him about this left side. He says, 'The crab apparently does not know the way. Left is the unfavourable side, left is sinister'. Sinister does indeed mean left and unfavourable. But the right side is also not good for the monster, because when it goes to the right it is touched by the wand and is killed. Now we come to his standing in between the angle of the monster's movement, a situation which at first glance he interpreted as incest. He says, 'As a matter of fact, I felt surrounded on either side like a hero who is going to fight a dragon'. So he himself realizes the hero motif.

But unlike the mythical hero he does not fight the dragon with a weapon, but with a wand. He says, 'From its effect on the monster it seems that it is a magical wand'. He certainly does dispose of the crab in a magical way. The wand is another mythological symbol. It often contains a sexual allusion, and sexual magic is a means of protection against danger. You may remember, too, how during the earthquake at Messina[8] nature produced certain instinctive reactions against the overwhelming destruction.

The wand is an instrument, and instruments in dreams mean what they actually are, the devices of man to concretize his will. For instance, a knife is my will to cut; when I use a spear I prolong my arm, with a rifle I can project my action and my influence to a great distance; with a telescope I do the same as regards my sight. An instrument is a mechanism which represents my will, my intelligence, my capability, and my cunning. Instruments in dreams symbolize an analogous psychological mechanism. Now this dreamer's instrument is a magic wand. He uses a marvellous thing by which he can spirit away the monster, that is, his lower nervous system. He can dispose of such nonsense in no time, and with no effort at all.

What does this actually mean? It means that he simply thinks that the danger does not exist. That is what is usually done. You simply think that a thing is not and then it is no more. That is how people behave who consist of the head only. They use their intellect in order to think things away; they reason them away. They say, 'This is nonsense, therefore it cannot be and therefore it is not'. That is what he also does. He simply reasons the monster away. He says, 'There is no such thing as a crab-lizard, there is no such thing as an opposing will; I get rid of it, I simply think it away. I think it is the mother with whom I want to commit incest, and that settles the whole thing, for I shall not do it'. I said, 'You have killed the animal – what do you think is the reason why you contemplate the animal for such a long time?' He said, 'Oh, well, yes, naturally it is marvellous how you can dispose of such a creature with such ease'. I said, 'Yes, indeed it is very marvellous!'

Then I told him what I thought of the situation. I said, 'Look here, the best way to deal with a dream is to think of yourself as a sort of ignorant child or ignorant youth, and to come to a two-million-year-old man or to the old mother of days and ask, 'Now, what do you think of me?' She would say to you, 'You have an ambitious plan, and that is foolish, because you run up against your own instincts. Your own restricted capabilities block the way. You want to abolish the obstacle by the magic of your thinking. You believe you can think it away by the artifices of your intellect, but it will be, believe me, matter for some afterthought'. And I also told him this: 'Your dreams contain a warning. You behave exactly like the engine-driver or like the Swiss who were foolhardy enough to run up against the enemy without any support behind them, and if you behave in the same way you will meet with a catastrophe'.

He was sure that such a point of view was much too serious. He was convinced that it is much more probable that dreams come from incompatible wishes and that he really had an unrealized incestuous wish which was at the bottom of this dream; that he was conscious now of this incestuous wish and had got rid of it and now could go to Leipzig. I said, 'Well then, bon voyage'. He did not return, he went on with his plans, and it took him just about three months to lose his position and go to the dogs. That was the end of him. He ran up against the fatal danger of that crab-lizard and would not understand the warning. But I do not want to make you too pessimistic. Sometimes there are people who really understand their dreams and draw conclusions which lead to a more favourable solution of their problems.

DISCUSSION

Dr Charles Brunton:

I do not know whether it is fair to ask about the dreams of someone who is not here, but I have a small daughter five and a half years old who has recently had two dreams which awakened her at night. The first dream occurred in the middle of August, and she told me this: 'I see a wheel, and it is rolling down a road and it burns me'. That was all I could get out of her. I wanted her to draw a picture of it the next day, but she did not want to be bothered, so I left it. The other dream was about a week ago, and this time it was 'a beetle that was pinching me'. That was all I could get about it. I do not know whether you would like to comment on them. The only thing I would like to add is that she knows the difference between a beetle and a crab. She is very fond of animals.

Professor Jung:

You have to consider that is is very difficult and not quite fair to comment on dreams of someone one does not know; but I will tell you as much as one can see from the symbolism. The beetle would, according to my idea, have to do with the sympathetic system. Therefore I should conclude from that dream that there are certain peculiar psychological processes going on in the child, which touch upon her sympathetic system, and this might arouse some intestinal or other abdominal disorder. The most cautious statement one could make would be to say that there is a certain accumulation of energy in the sympathetic system which causes slight disturbances. This is also borne out by the symbol of the fiery wheel. The wheel in her dream seems to be a sun-symbol, and in Tantric philosophy fire corresponds to the so-called *manipura chakra*, which is localized in the abdomen. In the prodromal symptoms of epilepsy you sometimes find the idea of a wheel revolving inside. This too expresses a manifestation of a sympathetic nature. The image of the revolving wheel reminds us of the wheel upon which Ixion was crucified. The dream of the little girl is an archetypal dream, one of those strange archetypal dreams children occasionally have.

I explain these archetypal dreams of children by the fact that when consciousness begins to dawn, when the child begins to feel that *he is*, he is still close to the original psychological world from which he has just emerged: a condition of deep unconsciousness. Therefore you find with many children an awareness of the contents of the collective unconscious, a fact which in some Eastern beliefs is interpreted as reminiscence of a former existence. Tibetan philosophy, for instance, speaks of the 'Bardo' existence and of the condition of the mind between death and birth.[9] The idea of former existence is a projection of the psychological condition of early childhood. Very young children still have an awareness of mythological contents, and if these contents remain conscious too long, the individual is threatened by an incapacity for adaptation; he is haunted by a constant yearning to remain with or to return to the original vision. There are very beautiful descriptions of these experiences by mystics and poets.

Usually at the age of four to six the veil of forgetfulness is drawn upon these experiences. However, I have seen cases of ethereal children, so to speak, who had an extraordinary awareness of these psychic facts and were living their life in archetypal dreams and could not adapt. Recently I saw a case of a little girl of ten who had some most amazing mythological dreams.[10] Her father consulted me about these dreams. I could not tell him what I thought because they contained an uncanny prognosis. The little girl died a year later of an infectious disease. She had never been born entirely.

Dr Leonard F. Browne:

I should like to ask Professor Jung a question with regard to the interpretation of the dreams he told us today. In view of the fact that the patient was unable to accept the interpretation, I should like to know whether that difficulty could have been overcome by some variation in the technique.

Professor Jung:

If I had had the intention of being a missionary, or a saviour, I should have used a clever trick. I should have said to the patient, 'Yes, that is the mother complex all right', and we would have gone on talking that kind of jargon for several months and perhaps in the end I would have swung him round. But I know from experience that such a thing is not good; you should not cheat people even for their good. I do not want to cheat people out of their mistaken faith. Perhaps it was better for that man to go to the dogs than to be saved by wrong means. I never hinder people. When somebody says, 'I am going to commit suicide if—', I say, 'If that is your intention, I have no objection'.

Dr Browne:

Did you have any evidence that the symptoms of mountain sickness were cured?

Professor Jung:

The patient lost his neurosis in going down in life. That man did not belong at a height of 6,000 feet; he belonged lower down. He became inferior instead of being neurotic. Once I talked to the head of a great institution in America for the education of criminal children, and was told about a very interesting experience. They have two categories of children. The majority of them, when they come to the institution, feel ever so much better, they develop very nicely and normally and they eventually grow out of whatever their original evil was. The other category, the minority, become hysterical when they try to be nice and normal. Those are the born criminals whom you cannot change. They are normal when they do wrong. We also do not feel quite right when we are behaving perfectly, we feel much better when we are doing a bit of wrong. That is because we are not perfect. The Hindus, when they build a temple, leave one corner unfinished; only the gods make something perfect, man never can. It is much better to know that one is not perfect, then one feels much better. So it is with these children, and so it is with our patients. It is wrong to cheat people out of their fate and to help them go beyond their level. If a man has it in him to be adapted, help him by all means; but if it is really his task not to be adapted, help him by all means not to be adapted, because then he is all right.

What would the world be like if all people were adapted? It would be boring beyond endurance. There must be some people who behave in the wrong way; they act as scapegoats and objects of interest for the normal ones. Think how grateful you are for detective novels and newspapers, so that you can say, 'Thank heaven I am not that fellow who has committed the crime, I am a perfectly innocent creature'. You feel satisfaction because the evil people have done it for you. This is the deeper meaning of the fact that Christ as the redeemer was crucified between two thieves. These thieves in their way were also redeemers of mankind, they were the scapegoats.

Question:

I would like to ask a question about the psychological functions, if that is not going too far back. In answering a question last night you said that there was no criterion for considering either of the four functions as being superior in itself and you further said that all the four functions would have to be equally differentiated in order to obtain full and adequate knowledge of the world. Do you mean, therefore, that it is possible in any given case for all the four functions to be equally differentiated or to be arrived at by education?

Professor Jung:

I do not believe that it is humanly possible to differentiate all four functions alike, otherwise we would be perfect like God, and that surely will not happen. There will always be a flaw in the crystal. We can never reach perfection. Moreover, if we could differentiate the four functions equally we should only make them into consciously disposable functions. Then we would lose the most precious connection with the unconscious through the inferior function, which is invariably the weakest; only through our feebleness and incapacity are we linked up with the unconscious, with the lower world of the instincts and with our fellow beings. Our virtues only enable us to be independent. There we do not need anybody, there we are kings; but in our inferiority we are linked up with mankind as well as with the world of our instincts. It would not even be an advantage to have all the functions perfect, because such a condition would amount to complete aloofness. I have no perfection craze. My principle is: for heaven's sake do not be perfect, but by all means try to be complete – whatever that means.

Question:

May I ask what it means to be complete? Will you enlarge upon that?

Professor Jung:

I must leave something to your own mental efforts. It is surely a most amusing enterprise, for instance, to think on your way home what it possibly means to be complete. We should not deprive people of the pleasure of discovering something. To be complete is a very great problem, and to talk of it is amusing, but to be it is the main thing.

Question:

How do you fit mysticism into your scheme?

Professor Jung:

Into what scheme?

Reply:

The scheme of psychology and the psyche.

Professor Jung:

Of course you should define what you mean by mysticism. Let us assume that you mean people who have mystical experience. Mystics are people who have a particularly vivid experience of the processes of the collective unconscious. Mystical experience is experience of archetypes.

Question:

Is there any difference between archetypal forms and mystical forms?

Professor Jung:

I make no distinction between them. If you study the phenomenology of mystical experience you will come across some very interesting things. For instance, you all know that our Christian heaven is a masculine heaven and that the feminine element is only tolerated. The Mother of God is not divine, she is only the arch-saint; she intercedes for us at the throne of God but she is not part of the Deity. She does not belong to the Trinity.

Now some Christian mystics have a different experience. For instance we have a Swiss mystic, Niklaus von der Flüe.[11] He experienced a God and a Goddess. Then there was a mystic of the thirteenth century, Guillaume de Diguileville, who wrote the *Pèlerinage de l'âme de Jésus Christ*.[12] Like Dante, he had a vision of the highest paradise as 'le ciel d'or', and there upon a throne one thousand times more bright than the sun sat le Roi, who is God himself, and beside him on a crystal throne of brownish hue, la Reine, presumably the Earth. This is a vision outside the Trinity idea, a mystical experience of an archetypal nature which includes the feminine principle. The Trinity is a dogmatic image based on an archetype of an exclusively masculine nature. In the Early Church the Gnostic interpretation of the Holy Ghost as feminine was declared a heresy.

Dogmatic images, such as the Trinity, are archetypes which have become abstract ideas. But there are a number of mystical experiences inside the Church whose archetypal character is still visible. Therefore they sometimes contain a heretical or pagan element. Remember, for instance, St Francis of Assisi. Only through the great diplomatic ability of Pope Boniface VIII could St Francis be assimilated into the Church. You have only to think of his relation to animals to understand the difficulty. Animals, like the whole of Nature, were taboo to the Church. Yet there are sacred animals like the Lamb, the Dove, and, in the Early Church, the Fish, which are worshipped.

Question:

Will Professor Jung give us his view on the psychological differences between the dissociation in hysteria and the dissociation in schizophrenia?

Professor Jung:

In hysteria the dissociated personalities are still in a sort of interrelation, so that you always get the impression of a total person. With a hysterical case you can establish a rapport, you get a feeling reaction from the whole person. There is only a superficial division between certain memory compartments, but the basic personality is always present. In the case of schizophrenia that is not so. There you encounter only fragments, there is nowhere a whole. Therefore, if you have a friend or a relative whom you have known well and who becomes insane, you will get a tremendous shock when you are confronted with a fragmentary personality which is completely split up. You can only deal with one fragment at a time; it is like a splinter of glass. You do not feel the continuity of the personality any longer. While with a hysterical case you think: if I could only wipe away that sort of obscuration or that sort of somnambulism then we should have the sum-total of the personality. But with schizophrenia it is a deep dissociation of personality; the fragments cannot come together any more.

Question:

Are there any more strictly psychological conceptions by which that difference can be expressed?

Professor Jung:

There are certain borderline cases where you can stitch the parts together if you can reintegrate the lost contents. I will tell you of a case I had. A woman had been twice in a lunatic asylum with a typical schizophrenic attack. When she was brought to me she was better, but still in a state of hallucination. I saw that it was possible to reach the split-off parts. Then I began to go through every detail of the experiences which she had had in the lunatic asylum with her; we went through all the voices and all the delusions, and I explained every fact to her so that she could associate them with her consciousness. I showed her what these unconscious contents were that came up during her insanity, and because she was an intelligent person, I gave her books to read so that she acquired a great deal of knowledge, chiefly mythological knowledge, by which she herself could stitch the parts together. The breaking lines were still there, of course, and whenever afterwards she had a new wave of disintegration I told her to try to draw or paint a picture of that particular situation in order to have a picture of the whole of herself which objectified her condition, and so she did. She brought me quite a number of pictures she had made, which had helped her whenever she felt she was falling apart again. In this way I have kept her afloat for about twelve years, and she has had no more attacks which necessitated her seclusion in an asylum. She could always manage to ward off the attacks by objectifying their contents. She told me, moreover, that when she had made such a picture she went to her books and read a chapter about some of its main features, in order to bring it into general connection with mankind, with what people know, with the collective consciousness, and then she felt right again. She said she felt adapted and she was no longer at the mercy of the collective unconscious.

All cases are not as accessible as that one, as you will realize. I cannot cure schizophrenia in principle. Occasionally by great good chance I can synthetize the fragments. But I do not like to do it because it is frightfully difficult work.

NOTES

1 [Cf. 'On the Importance of the Unconscious in Psychopathology', and 'On Psychological Understanding', both delivered in 1914 (C.W., vol. 3).]
2 For example, the figures of *anima* and *animus*. [See *Two Essays on Analytical Psychology* (C.W., vol. 7), pars. 296ff.]
3 'The Familial Constellations' (C.W., vol. 2) and 'The Significance of the Father in the Destiny of the Individual' (C.W., vol. 4), pars. 698–702.
4 'On the Practical Use of Dream Analysis' (C.W., vol. 16). [Also 'General Aspects of Dream Psychology' and 'On the Nature of Dreams' (C.W., vol. 8).]
5 [The reference is to Wilhelm Wundt, of Leipzig (1832–1920).]

6   *Psychological Types*, Def. 48. See also *Two Essays*, pars. 296ff. [Also *Aion* (C.W., vol. 9, ii), ch. 3.]

7   [E.g., *Symbols of Transformation*, Part II, ch. V, especially par. 395.]

8   [The reference is to the disaster of 1908, when 90 per cent of the Sicilian city was destroyed, with a loss of 60,000 lives.]

9   Cf. W. Y. Evans-Wentz, *The Tibetan Book of the Dead*.

10   [Cf. Jung, 'Approaching the Unconscious', in *Man and His Symbols*, pp. 69ff. The case is also discussed in Jacobi, *Complex/Archetype/Symbol*, pp. 139ff.]

11   ['Brother Klaus' (C.W., vol. 11).]

12   [*Psychology and Alchemy* (C.W., vol. 12), pars. 315ff.]

LECTURE FOUR

The Chairman (Dr Emanuel Miller):

I shall not take any of Professor Jung's time away from you but will merely express my great pleasure at the opportunity of being Chairman this evening. Only I am put to a grave disadvantage: I have not been able to attend the previous lectures and therefore I do not know to what depths of the unconscious Professor Jung has already led you, but I think he is going to continue tonight the presentation of his method of dream-analysis.

Professor Jung:

The interpretation of a profound dream, such as our last one was, is never sufficient when it is left in the personal sphere. This dream contains an archetypal image, and that is always an indication that the psychological situation of the dreamer extends beyond the mere personal layer of the unconscious. His problem is no more entirely a personal affair, but something which touches upon the problems of mankind in general. The symbol of the monster is an indication of this. This symbol brings up the hero myth, and furthermore the association with the battle of St Jacob, which characterizes the localization of the scene, appeals also to a general interest.

The ability to apply a general point of view is of great therapeutic importance. Modern therapy is not much aware of this, but in ancient medicine it was well known that the raising of the personal disease to a higher and more impersonal level had a curative effect. In ancient Egypt, for instance, when a man was bitten by a snake, the priest-physician was called in, and he took from the temple library the manuscript about the myth of Rā and his mother

Isis, and recited it. Isis had made a poisonous worm and hidden it in the sand, and the god Rā had stepped on the serpent and was bitten by it, so that he suffered terrible pain and was threatened with death. Therefore the gods caused Isis to work a spell which drew the poison out of him.[1] The idea was that the patient would be so impressed by this narrative that he would be cured. To us this sounds quite impossible. We could not imagine that the reading of a story from Grimm's Fairy Tales, for instance, would cure typhoid fever or pneumonia. But we only take into account our rational modern psychology. To understand the effect we have to consider the psychology of the ancient Egyptians, which was quite different. And yet those people were not so very different. Even with us certain things can work miracles; sometimes spiritual consolation or psychological influence alone can cure, or at least will help to cure an illness. And of course it is all the more so with a person on a more primitive level and with a more archaic psychology.

In the East a great amount of practical therapy is built upon this principle of raising the mere personal ailment into a generally valid situation, and ancient Greek medicine also worked with the same method. Of course the collective image or its application has to be in accordance with the particular psychological condition of the patient. The myth or legend arises from the archetypal material which is constellated by the disease, and the psychological effect consists in connecting the patient with the general human meaning of his particular situation. Snakebite, for instance, is an archetypal situation, therefore you find it as a motif in any number of tales. If the archetypal situation underlying the illness can be expressed in the right way the patient is cured. If no adequate expression is found, the individual is thrown back upon himself, into the isolation of being ill; he is alone and has no connection with the world. But if he is shown that his particular ailment is not his ailment only, but a general ailment – even a god's ailment – he is in the company of men and gods, and this knowledge produces a healing effect. Modern spiritual therapy uses the same principle: pain or illness is compared with the sufferings of Christ, and this idea gives consolation. The individual is lifted out of his miserable loneliness and represented as undergoing a heroic meaningful fate which is ultimately good for the whole world, like the suffering and death of a god. When an ancient Egyptian was shown that he was undergoing the fate of Rā, the sun-god, he was immediately ranked with the Pharaoh, who was the son and representative of the gods, and so the ordinary man was a god himself, and this brought such a release of energy that we can understand quite well how he was lifted out of his pain. In a particular frame of mind people can endure a great deal. Primitives can walk on glowing coals and inflict the most terrible injuries on themselves under certain circumstances without feeling any pain. And so it is quite likely that an impressive and adequate symbol can mobilize the forces of the unconscious to such an extent that even the nervous system becomes affected and the body begins to react in a normal way again.

In the case of psychological suffering, which always isolates the individual from the herd of so-called normal people, it is also of the greatest importance to understand that the conflict is not a personal failure only, but at the same time a suffering common to all and a problem with which the whole epoch is burdened. This general point of view lifts the individual out of himself and connects him with humanity. The suffering does not even have to be a neurosis; we have the same feeling in very ordinary circumstances. If for instance you live in a well-to-do community, and you suddenly lose all your money, your natural reaction will be to think that it is terrible and shameful and that you are the only one who is such an ass as to lose his money. But if everybody loses his money it is quite another matter and you feel reconciled to it. When other people are in the same hole as I am I feel much better. If a man is lost in the desert or quite alone on a glacier, or if he is the responsible leader of a group of men in a precarious situation, he will feel terrible. But when he is a soldier in a whole battalion that is lost, he will join the rest in cheering and making jokes, and will not realize the danger. The danger is not less, but the individual feels quite differently about it in a group than when he has to face it alone.

Whenever archetypal figures appear in dreams, especially in the later stages of analysis, I explain to the patient that his case is not particular and personal, but that his psychology is approaching a level which is universally human. That outlook is very important, because a neurotic feels tremendously isolated and ashamed of his neurosis. But if he knows his problem to be general and not merely personal, it makes all the difference. In the case of our dreamer, if I had been going on with the treatment I would have called the patient's attention to the fact that the motif in his last dream was a general human situation. He himself in his associations had realized the hero-dragon conflict.

The hero's fight with the dragon, as the symbol of a typical human situation, is a very frequent mythological motif. One of the most ancient literary expressions of it is the Babylonian Creation Myth, where the hero-god Marduk fights the dragon Tiamat. Marduk is the spring-god and Tiamat is the mother-dragon, the primordial chaos. Marduk kills her and splits her in two parts. From one half he makes the heavens and from the other he makes the earth.[2]

A more striking parallel to our case is the great Babylonian epos of Gilgamesh.[3] Gilgamesh is really an *arriviste par excellence*, a man of ambitious plans, like our dreamer, and a great king and hero. All the men are working for him like slaves to build a town with mighty walls. The women feel neglected and complain to the gods about their reckless tyrant. So the gods decide that something has to be done about it. Translated into psychological language this means: Gilgamesh is using his consciousness only, his head has wings and is detached from the body, and his body is going to say something about it. It will react with a neurosis, that is, by constellating a very opposite factor. How is this neurosis described in the poem? The gods decide to 'call up', that is to make, a man like Gilgamesh. They create Enkidu; yet he is in some ways different. The hair of his head is long; he looks like a cave-man; and he lives with the wild animals in the plains and drinks from the water-wells of the gazelles. Gilgamesh, being normal so far, has a perfectly normal dream about the intention of the gods. He dreams that a star falls down on his back, a star like a mighty warrior, and Gilgamesh is wrestling with him but cannot shake himself free. Finally he overcomes him and puts him down at his mother's feet, and the mother 'makes him equal' to Gilgamesh. The mother is a wise woman and interprets the dream for Gilgamesh so that he is ready to meet the danger. Enkidu is meant to fight Gilgamesh and bring him down but Gilgamesh in a very clever way makes him his friend. He has conquered the reaction of his unconscious by cunning and will-power and he persuades his opponent that they are really friends and that they can work together. Now things are going worse than ever.

Although right in the beginning Enkidu has an oppressive dream, a vision of the underworld where the dead live, Gilgamesh is preparing for a great adventure. Like heroes, Gilgamesh and Enkidu start out together to overcome Humbaba, a terrible monster whom the gods have made guardian of their sanctuary on the cedar mountain. His voice roars like the tempest, and everybody who approaches the wood is overcome by weakness. Enkidu is brave and very strong, but he is nervous about the enterprise. He is depressed by bad dreams and pays a lot of attention to them, like the inferior man in ourselves whom we ridicule when that inferior part of ourselves feels super-stitious about certain dates, and so on; the inferior man nevertheless continues to be nervous about certain things. Enkidu is very superstitious, he has had bad dreams on the way to the forest and has forebodings that things will go wrong. But Gilgamesh interprets the dreams optimistically. Again the reaction of the unconscious is cheated, and they succeed in bringing back Humbaba's head triumphantly to their city.

Now the gods decide to interfere, or rather it is a goddess, Ishtar, who tries to defeat Gilgamesh. The ultimate principle of the unconscious is the Eternal Feminine, and Ishtar, with true feminine cunning, makes wonderful prom-ises to Gilgamesh if he will become her lover: he would be like a god and his power and wealth would increase beyond measure. But Gilgamesh does not believe a word of it, he refuses with insulting words and reproaches her for all her faithlessness and cruelty towards her lovers. Ishtar in her rage and fury persuades the gods to create an enormous bull, which descends from the heavens and devastates the country. A great fight begins, and hundreds of men are killed by the poisonous breath of the divine bull. But again Gilgamesh, with the help of Enkidu, slays him, and the victory is celebrated.

Ishtar, overcome by rage and pain, descends to the wall of the city, and now Enkidu himself commits an outrage against her. He curses her and throws the member of the dead bull in her face. This is the climax, and now the peripeteia sets in. Enkidu has more dreams of an ominous nature and becomes seriously ill and dies.

This means that the conscious separates from the unconscious altogether; the unconscious withdraws from the field, and Gilgamesh is now alone and overcome with grief. He can hardly accept the loss of his friend, but what torments him most is the fear of death. He has seen his friend die and is faced with the fact that he is mortal too. One more desire tortures him – to secure immortality. He sets out heroically to find the medicine against death, because he knows of an old man, his ancestor, who has eternal life and who lives far away in the West. So the journey to the underworld, the Nekyia, begins, and he travels to the West like the sun, through the door of the heavenly mountain. He overcomes enormous difficulties, and even the gods do not oppose his plan, although they tell him that he will seek in vain. Finally he comes to his destination and persuades the old man to tell him of the remedy. At the bottom of the sea he acquires the magic herb of immortality, the *pharmakon athanasias*, and he is bringing the herb home. Although he is tired of travelling he is full of joy because he has the wonderful medicine and does not need to be afraid of death any more. But while he is refreshing himself by bathing in a pool, a snake smells out the herb of immortality and steals it from him. After his return, he takes up new plans for the fortification of his city, but he finds no peace. He wants to know what happens to man after death and he finally succeeds in evoking Enkidu's spirit, which comes up from a hole in the earth and gives Gilgamesh very melancholy information. With this the epos ends. The ultimate victory is won by the cold-blooded animal.

There are quite a number of dreams recorded from antiquity with parallel motifs, and I will give you a short example of how our colleagues of old – the dream interpreters of the first century A.D. – proceeded. The story is told by Flavius Josephus in his history of the Jewish war,[4] where he also records the destruction of Jerusalem.

There was a Tetrarch of Palestine by the name of Archelaos, a Roman governor who was very cruel and who, like practically all of those provincial governors, regarded his position as an opportunity to enrich himself and steal what he could lay his hands on. Therefore a delegation was sent to the emperor Augustus to complain about him. This was in the tenth year of Archelaos' governorship. About this time he had a dream in which he saw nine big ripe ears of wheat which were eaten up by hungry oxen. Archelaos was alarmed and instantly called in his court 'psychoanalyst'. But the 'psycho-analyst' did not know what the dream meant, or he was afraid to tell the truth and wriggled out of it. Archelaos called in other 'psychoanalysts' for consulta-tion, and they in the same way refused to know anything about the dream.

But there was a peculiar sect of people, the Essenes or Therapeutai, with more independent minds. They lived in Egypt and near the Dead Sea, and it is not impossible that John the Baptist as well as Simon Magus belonged to such circles. So as a last resort a man called Simon the Essene was sent for, and he told Archelaos: 'The ears of wheat signify the years of your reign, and the oxen the change of things. The nine years are fulfilled and there will be a great change in your fate. The hungry oxen mean your destruction'. In those countries such a dream-image would be perfectly understandable. The fields have to be guarded carefully against foraging cattle. There is little grass, and it is a catastrophe when during the night the oxen break through the fence into the field and trample down and eat the growing grain, so that in the morning the whole bread of a year is gone. Now for the confirmation of the interpre-tation. A few days later a Roman ambassador arrived to investigate, dismissed Archelaos, took all his property from him, and exiled him to Gaul.

Archelaos was married, and his wife, Glaphyra, also had a dream. Naturally she was impressed by what had happened to her husband. She dreamt of her first husband – Archelaos was her third marriage – who had been disposed of in a very impolite way: he had been murdered, and Archelaos was most prob-ably the murderer. Things were a bit rough in those days. This former husband, Alexandros, appeared to her in the dream and blamed her for her conduct and told her that he was going to take her back into his household. Simon did not interpret this dream, so the analysis is left to our discretion. The impor-tant fact is that Alexandros was dead, and that Glaphyra saw the dead husband in her dream. This, of course, in those days, meant the ghost of that person. So when he told her that he was going to take her back to his household it signified that he was going to fetch her to Hades. And indeed, a few days later she committed suicide.

The way the dream-interpreter proceeded with the dream of Archelaos was very sensible. He understood the dream exactly as we would, although these dreams are of a much simpler nature than most of our dreams. I have noticed that dreams are as simple or as complicated as the dreamer is himself, only they are always a little bit ahead of the dreamer's consciousness. I do not understand my own dreams any better than any of you, for they are always somewhat beyond my grasp and I have the same trouble with them as anyone who knows nothing about dream-interpretation. Knowledge is no advantage when it is a matter of one's own dreams.

Another interesting parallel to our case is the story you all know in the fourth chapter of the Book of Daniel.[5] When the king Nebuchadnezzar had conquered the whole of Mesopotamia and Egypt, he thought he was very great indeed because he possessed the whole known world. Then he had the typical dream of the *arriviste* who has climbed too high. He dreamed of an enormous tree growing up to heaven and casting a shadow over the whole earth. But then a watcher and holy one from heaven ordered the tree to be hewn down, and his branches cut off, and his leaves shaken, so that only his stump remained: and that he should live with the beasts and his human heart be taken from him and a beast's heart given to him.

Of course all the astrologers and wise men and dream-interpreters refused to understand the dream. Only Daniel, who already in the second chapter had proved himself a courageous analyst – he even had a vision of a dream which Nebuchadnezzar could not remember – understood its meaning. He warned the king to repent of his avarice and injustice, otherwise the dream would come true. But the king went on as before, very proud of his power. Then a voice from heaven cursed him and repeated the prophecy of the dream. And it all happened as foretold. Nebuchadnezzar was cast out to the beasts and he became like an animal himself. He ate grass as the oxen and his body was wet with the dew of heaven, his hair grew long like eagles' feathers and his nails like birds' claws. He was turned back into a primitive man and all his conscious reason was taken away because he had misused it. He regressed even further back than the primitive and became completely inhuman; he was Humbaba, the monster, himself. All this symbolized a complete regressive degeneration of a man who has overreached himself.

His case, like our patient's, is the eternal problem of the successful man who has overreached himself and is contradicted by his unconscious. The contradiction is first shown in the dreams and, if not accepted, must be experienced in reality in a fatal way. These historical dreams, like all dreams, have a *compensatory function*: they are an indication – a symptom, if you prefer to say so – that the individual is at variance with unconscious conditions, that somewhere he has deviated from his natural path. Somewhere he has fallen a victim to his ambition and his ridiculous designs, and, if he does not pay attention, the gap will widen and he will fall into it, as our patient has.

I want to emphasize that it is not safe to interpret a dream without going into careful detail as to the context. Never apply any theory, but always ask the patient how *he* feels about his dream-images. For dreams are always about a particular problem of the individual about which he has a wrong conscious judgment. The dreams are the reaction to our conscious attitude in the same way that the body reacts when we overeat or do not eat enough or when we ill-treat it in some other way. *Dreams are the natural reaction of the self-regulating psychic system.* This formulation is the nearest I can get to a theory about the structure and function of dreams. I hold that dreams are just as manifold and unpredictable and incalculable as a person you observe during the day. If you watch an individual at one moment and then at another you will see and hear the most varied reactions, and it is exactly the same with dreams. In our dreams we are just as many-sided as in our daily life, and just as you cannot form a theory about those many aspects of the conscious personality you cannot make a general theory of dreams. Otherwise we would have an almost divine knowledge of the human mind, which we certainly do not possess. We know precious little about it, therefore we call the things we do not know unconscious.

But today I am going to contradict myself and break all my rules. I am going to interpret a single dream, not one out of a series; moreover I do not know the dreamer, and further, I am not in possession of the associations. Therefore I am interpreting the dream arbitrarily. There is a justification for this procedure. If a dream is clearly formed of personal material you have to get the individual associations; but if the dream is chiefly a mythological structure – a difference which is obvious at once – then it speaks a universal language, and you or I can supply parallels with which to construct the context as well as anybody else, always provided we possess the necessary knowledge. For instance, when the dream takes up the hero-dragon conflict, everybody has something to say about it, because we have all read fairytales and legends and know something of heroes and dragons. On the collective level of dreams there is practically no difference in human beings, while there is all the difference on the personal level.

The main substance of the dream I am going to speak of is mythological. Here we are confronted with the question: Under what conditions does one have mythological dreams? With us they are rather rare, as our conscious-ness is to a great extent detached from the underlying archetypal mind. Mythological dreams therefore are felt by us as a very alien element. But this is not so with a mentality nearer to the primordial psyche. Primitives pay great attention to such dreams and call them 'big dreams' in contradistinction to ordinary ones. They feel that they are important and contain a general meaning. Therefore in a primitive community the dreamer feels bound to announce a big dream to the assembly of men, and a palaver is held over it. Such dreams were also announced to the Roman Senate. There is a story of a senator's daughter in the first century B.C. who dreamed that the goddess Minerva had appeared to her and complained that the Roman people were neglecting her temple. The lady felt obliged to report the dream to the Senate, and the Senate voted a certain sum of money for the restoration of the temple. A similar case is told of Sophocles, when a precious golden vessel had been stolen from the temple of Herakles. The god appeared to Sophocles in a dream and told him the name of the thief.[6] After the third repetition of the dream, Sophocles felt obliged to inform the Areopagus. The man in question was seized, and in the course of the investigation he confessed and brought back the vessel. These mythological or collective dreams have a character which forces people instinctively to tell them. This instinct is quite appropriate, because such dreams do not belong to the individual; they have a collective meaning. They are true in themselves in general, and in particular they are true for people in certain circumstances. That is the reason why in antiquity and in the Middle Ages dreams were held in great esteem. It was felt that they expressed a collective human truth.

Now I will tell you the dream. It was sent to me by a colleague of mine years ago with a few remarks about the dreamer. My colleague was an alienist at a clinic, and the patient was a distinguished young Frenchman, twenty-two years of age, highly intelligent, and very aesthetic. He had travelled in Spain and had come back with a depression which was diagnosed as manic-depressive insanity, depressive form. The depression was not very bad, but bad enough for him to be sent to the clinic. After six months he was released from confinement, and a few months later he committed suicide. He was no longer under the depression, which was practically cured; he committed suicide apparently in a state of calm reasoning. We shall understand from the dream why he committed suicide. This is the dream, and it occurred at the beginning of the depression:

Underneath the great cathedral of Toledo there is a cistern filled with water which has a subterranean connection with the river Tagus, which skirts the city. This cistern is a small dark room. In the water there is a huge serpent whose eyes sparkle like jewels. Near it there is a golden bowl containing a golden dagger. This dagger is the key to Toledo, and its owner commands full power over the city. The dreamer knows the serpent to be the friend and protector of B— C—, a young friend of his who is present. B— C— puts his naked foot into the serpent's jaws. The serpent licks it in a friendly way and B— C— enjoys playing with the serpent; he has no fear of it because he is a child without guile. In the dream B— C— appears to be about the age of seven; he had indeed been a friend of the dreamer's early youth. Since this time, the dream says, the serpent has been forgotten and nobody dared to descend into its haunts.

This part is a sort of introduction, and now the real action begins.

The dreamer is alone with the serpent. He talks to it respectfully, but without fear. The serpent tells the dreamer that Spain belongs to him as he is B— C—'s friend, and asks him to give back the boy. The dreamer refuses to do this and promises instead that he himself will descend into the darkness of the cave to be the friend of the serpent. But then he changes his mind, and instead of fulfilling his promise he decides to send another friend, a Mr S—, to the serpent. This friend is descended from the Spanish Moors, and to risk the descent into the cistern he has to recover the original courage of his race. The dreamer advises him to get the sword with the red hilt which is to be found in the weapons factory on the other bank of the Tagus. It is said to be a very ancient sword, dating back to the old Phocaeans.[7] S— gets the sword and descends into the cistern, and the dreamer tells him to pierce his left palm with the sword. S— does so, but he is not able to keep his countenance in the powerful presence of the serpent. Overcome by pain and fear, he cries out and

staggers upstairs again without having taken the dagger. Thus S— cannot hold Toledo, and the
dreamer could do nothing about it and had to let him stay there as a mere wall decoration.

That is the end of the dream. The original of course is in French. Now for
the context. We have certain hints as to these friends. B— C— is a friend of
the dreamer's early youth, a little bit older than himself, and he projected
everything that was wonderful and charming into this boy and made him a
sort of hero. But he lost sight of him later; perhaps the boy died. S— is a
friend of more recent date. He is said to be descended from the Spanish
Moors. I do not know him personally, but I know his family. It is a very old
and honourable family from the South of France, and the name might easily
be a Moorish name. The dreamer knew this legend about the family of S—.

As I told you, the dreamer had recently been to Spain and of course had
seen Toledo, and he had the dream after he got back and had been taken
to the clinic. He was in a bad state, practically in despair, and he could not
help telling the dream to his doctor. My colleague did not know what to
do with it, but he felt an urge to send me the dream because he felt it to be
very important. But at the time I received the dream I could not understand
it. Nevertheless I had the feeling that if I had known something more
about such dreams, and if I could have handled the case myself, I might have
been able to help the young man and his suicide might not have occurred.
Since then I have seen many cases of a similar nature. Often one can turn a
difficult corner by a real understanding of dreams like this one. With such
a sensitive, refined individual who had studied the history of art and was
an unusually artistic and intelligent person, one must be exceedingly careful.
Banalities are no use in such a case; one has to be serious and enter into the
real material.

We make no mistake when we assume that the dreamer has picked out
Toledo for a particular reason – both as the object of his trip and of his dream;
and the dream brings up material which practically everybody would have
who had seen Toledo with the same mental disposition, the same education
and refinement of aesthetic perception and knowledge. Toledo is an extremely
impressive city. It contains one of the most marvellous Gothic cathedrals of
the world. It is a place with an immensely old tradition; it is the old Roman
Toletum, and for centuries has been the seat of the Cardinal Archbishop and
Primate of Spain. From the sixth to the eighth century it was the capital of
the Visigoths; from the eighth to the eleventh it was a provincial capital of the
Moorish kingdom; and from the eleventh to the sixteenth century it was the
capital of Castile. The cathedral of Toledo, being such an impressive and beautiful building, naturally suggests all that it represents: the greatness, the
power, the splendour, and the mystery of medieval Christianity, which found
its essential expression in the Church. Therefore the cathedral is the embodi-
ment, the incarnation, of the spiritual kingdom, for in the Middle Ages the

world was ruled by the Emperor and by God. So the cathedral expresses the Christian philosophy or *Weltanschauung* of the Middle Ages.

The dream says that underneath the cathedral there is a mysterious place, which in reality is not in tune with a Christian church. What is beneath a cathedral of that age? There is always the so-called under-church or crypt. You have probably seen the great crypt at Chartres; it gives a very good idea of the mysterious character of a crypt. The crypt at Chartres was previously an old sanctuary with a well, where the worship of a virgin was celebrated – not of the Virgin Mary, as is done now – but of a Celtic goddess. Under every Christian church of the Middle Ages there is a secret place where in old times the mysteries were celebrated. What we now call the sacraments of the Church were the mysteria of early Christianity. In Provençal the crypt is called *le musset*, which means a secret; the word perhaps originates from *mysteria* and could mean mystery-place. In Aosta, where they speak a Provençal dialect, there is a *musset* under the cathedral.

The crypt is probably taken over from the cult of Mithras. In Mithraism the main religious ceremony took place in a vault half sunk into the earth, and the community remained separated in the main church above. There were peepholes so that they could see and hear the priests and the elect ones chanting and celebrating their rites below, but they were not admitted to them. That was a privilege for the initiates. In the Christian church the separation of the baptistry from the main body of the building derives from the same idea, for baptism as well as the communion were mysteria of which one could not speak directly. One had to use a sort of allegorical allusion so as not to betray the secrets. The mystery also attached to the name of Christ, which therefore was not allowed to be mentioned; instead, he was referred to by the name of Ichthys, the Fish. You have probably seen reproductions of very early Christian paintings where Christ appears as the Fish. This secrecy connected with the holy name is probably the reason why the name of Christ is not mentioned in an early Christian document of about A.D. 140 known as *The Shepherd* of Hermas,[8] which was an important part of the body of Christian literature recognized by the Church till about the fifth century. The writer of this book of visions, Hermas, is supposed to have been the brother of the Roman bishop Pius. The spiritual teacher who appears to Hermas is called the Poimen, the Shepherd, and not the Christ.

The idea of the crypt or mystery-place leads us to something below the Christian *Weltanschauung*, something older than Christianity, like the pagan well below the cathedral at Chartres, or like an antique cave inhabited by a serpent. The well with the serpent is of course not an actual fact which the dreamer saw when he travelled in Spain. This dream-image is not an individual experience and can therefore only be paralleled by archaeological and mythological knowledge. I have to give you a certain amount of that parallelism so that you can see in what context or tissue such a symbolical arrangement appears when looked at in the light of comparative research work. You know that every church still has its baptismal font. This was originally the piscina, the pond, in which the initiates were bathed or symbolically drowned. After a figurative death in the baptismal bath they came out transformed *quasi modo geniti*, as reborn ones. So we can assume that the crypt or baptismal font has the meaning of a place of terror and death and also of rebirth, a place where dark initiations take place.

The serpent in the cave is an image which often occurs in antiquity. It is important to realize that in classical antiquity, as in other civilizations, the serpent not only was an animal that aroused fear and represented danger, but also signified healing. Therefore Asklepios, the god of physicians, is connected with the serpent; you all know his emblem which is still in use. In the temples of Asklepios, the Asklepieia, which were the ancient clinics, there was a hole in the ground, covered by a stone, and in that hole lived the sacred serpent. There was a slot in the stone through which the people who came to the place of healing threw down the fee for the doctors. The snake was at the same time the cashier of the clinic and collector of gifts that were thrown down into its cave. During the great pestilence in the time of Diocletian the famous serpent of the Asklepieion at Epidaurus was brought to Rome as an antidote to the epidemic. It represented the god himself.

The serpent is not only the god of healing; it also has the quality of wisdom and prophecy. The fountain of Castalia at Delphi was originally inhabited by a python. Apollo fought and overcame the python, and from that time Delphi was the seat of the famous oracle and Apollo its god, until he left half his powers to Dionysus, who later came in from the East. In the underworld, where the spirits of the dead live, snakes and water are always together, as we can read in Aristophanes' *The Frogs*. The serpent in legend is often replaced by the dragon; the Latin *draco* simply means snake. A particularly suggestive parallel to our dream symbol is a Christian legend of the fifth century about St Sylvester:[9] there was a terrible dragon in a cave under the Tarpeian rock in Rome to whom virgins were sacrificed. Another legend says that the dragon was not a real one but artificial, and that a monk went down to prove it was not real and when he got down to the cave he found that the dragon had a sword in his mouth and his eyes consisted of sparkling jewels.

Very often these caves, like the cave of Castalia, contain springs. These springs played a very important role in the cult of Mithras, from which many elements of the early Church originated. Porphyry relates that Zoroaster, the founder of the Persian religion, dedicated to Mithras a cave containing many springs. Those of you who have been to Germany and seen the Saalburg near Frankfurt will have noticed the spring near the grotto of Mithras. The cult of Mithras is always connected with a spring. There is a beautiful Mithraeum in

Provence which has a large piscina with wonderful crystal-clear water, and in the background a rock on which is carved the Mithras Tauroktonos – the bull-killing Mithras. These sanctuaries were always a great scandal to the early Christians. They hated all these natural arrangements because they were no friends of nature. In Rome a Mithraeum has been discovered ten feet below the surface of the Church of San Clemente. It is still in good condition but filled with water, and when it is pumped out it fills again. It is always under water because it adjoins a spring which floods the interior. The spring has never been found. We know of other religious ideas in antiquity, for instance of the Orphic cult, which always associate the underworld with water.

This material will give you an idea that the serpent in the cave full of water is an image that was generally known and played a great role in antiquity. As you have noticed, I have chosen all my examples exclusively from antiquity; I could have chosen other parallels from other civilizations, and you would find it was the same. The water in the depths represents the unconscious. In the depths as a rule is a treasure guarded by a serpent or a dragon; in our dream the treasure is the golden bowl with the dagger in it. In order to recover the treasure the dragon has to be overcome. The treasure is of a very mysterious nature. It is connected with the serpent in a strange way; the peculiar nature of the serpent denotes the character of the treasure as though the two things were one. Often there is a golden snake with the treasure. Gold is something that everyone is seeking, so we could say that it looks as if the serpent himself were the great treasure, the source of immense power. In early Greek myths, for instance, the dweller in the cave is a hero, such as Cecrops, the founder of Athens. Above he is half man and half woman, a hermaphrodite, but the lower part of his body is a serpent; he is clearly a monster. The same is said of Erechtheus, another mythical king of Athens.

That prepares us a little for understanding the golden bowl and the dagger in our dream. If you have seen Wagner's Parsifal you know that the bowl corresponds to the Grail and the dagger to the spear and that the two belong together; they are the male and the female principle which form the union of opposites. The cave or underworld represents a layer of the unconscious where there is no discrimination at all, not even a distinction between the male and the female, which is the first differentiation primitives make. They distinguish objects in this way, as we still do occasionally. Some keys, for instance, have a hole in the front, and some are solid. They are often called male and female keys. You know the Italian tiled roofs. The convex tiles are placed above and the concave ones underneath. The upper ones are called monks and the under ones the nuns. This is not an indecent joke to the Italians, but the quintessence of discrimination.

When the unconscious brings together the male and the female, things become utterly indistinguishable and we cannot say any more whether they are male or female, just as Cecrops came from such a mythical distance that one could not say whether he was man or woman, human or serpent. So we see that the bottom of the cistern in our dream is characterized by a complete union of opposites. This is the primordial condition of things, and at the same time a most ideal achievement, because it is the union of elements eternally opposed. Conflict has come to rest, and everything is still or once again in the original state of indistinguishable harmony. You find the same idea in ancient Chinese philosophy. The ideal condition is named Tao, and it consists of the complete harmony between heaven and earth. Figure 13 represents the symbol for Tao. On one side it is white with a black spot, and on the other it is black with a white spot. The white side is the hot, dry, fiery principle, the south; the black side is the cold, humid, dark principle, the north. The condition of Tao is the beginning of the world where nothing has yet begun – and it is also the condition to be achieved by the attitude of superior wisdom. The idea of the union of the two opposite principles, of male and female, is an archetypal image. I once had a very nice example of its still-living primitive form. When on military duty with the army during the war, I was with the mountain artillery, and the soldiers had to dig a deep hole for the position of a heavy gun. The soil was very refractory, and they cursed a good deal while they were digging up the heavy blocks. I was sitting hidden behind a rock, smoking my pipe and listening to what they said. One man said: 'Now, damn it all, we have dug into the depths of this blooming old valley where the old lake-dwellers lived and where father and mother are still sleeping together'. That is the same idea, very naïvely expressed. A Negro myth says that the primordial man and the primordial woman were sleeping together in the calabash; they were quite unconscious until they found they were torn asunder and what was in between was the son. Man was in between, and from that time they were separated, and then they knew each other. The original condition of absolute unconsciousness is expressed as a completely restful condition where nothing happens.

When the dreamer comes to these symbols he reaches the layer of complete unconsciousness, which is represented as the greatest treasure. It

Figure 13 Tao

is the central motif in Wagner's *Parsifal* that the spear should be restored to the Grail because they belong eternally together. This union is a symbol of complete fulfilment – eternity before and after the creation of the world, a dormant condition. That is probably the thing which the desire of man is seeking. That is why he ventures into the cave of the dragon, to find that condition where consciousness and the unconscious are so completely united that he is neither conscious nor unconscious. Whenever the two are too much separated, consciousness seeks to unite them again by going down into the depths where they once were one. Thus you find in Tantric Yoga or Kundalini Yoga an attempt to reach the condition where Shiva is in eternal union with Shakti. Shiva is the eternally unextended point, and he is encircled by the female principle, Shakti, in the form of a serpent.

I could give you many more instances of this idea. It played a great role in the secret tradition of the Middle Ages. In medieval alchemical texts there are pictures of the process of the union of Sol and Luna, the male and the female principle. We have traces of an analogous symbolism in Christian reports about the ancient mysteries. There is a report by a Bishop Asterios about Eleusis, and it says that every year the priest made the *katabasis* or descent into the cave. And the priest of Apollo and the priestess of Demeter, the earth mother, celebrated the *hierosgamos*, the sacred nuptials, for the fertilization of the earth. This is a Christian statement which is not substantiated. The initiates of the Eleusinian mysteries kept the strictest secrecy; if they betrayed anything, they were punished with death. So we have practically no knowledge of their rites. We know, on the other hand, that during the mysteries of Demeter certain obscenities took place because they were thought good for the fertility of the earth. The distinguished ladies of Athens assembled, with the priestess of Demeter presiding. They had a good meal and plenty of wine and afterwards performed the rite of the *aischrologia*. That is, they had to tell indecent jokes. This was considered a religious duty because it was good for the fertility of the next season.[10] A similar rite took place in Bubastis in Egypt at the time of the Isis mysteries. The inhabitants of the villages on the upper Nile came down in parties, and the women on the barges used to expose themselves to the women on the banks of the Nile. It was probably done for the same reason as the *aischrologia* – to ensure the fertility of the earth. You can read about it in Herodotus.[11] In southern Germany as late as the nineteenth century, in order to increase the fertility of the soil, the peasant used to take his wife to his fields and have intercourse with her in a furrow. This is called sympathetic magic.

The bowl is a vessel that receives or contains, and is therefore female. It is a symbol of the body which contains the anima, the breath and liquid of life, while the dagger has piercing, penetrating qualities and is therefore male. It cuts, it discriminates and divides, and so is a symbol of the masculine Logos principle.

In our dream the dagger is said to be the key to Toledo. The idea of the key is often associated with the mysteries in the cave. In the cult of Mithras there is a peculiar kind of god, the key god Aion, whose presence could not be explained; but I think it is quite understandable. He is represented with the winged body of a man and the head of a lion, and he is encoiled by a snake which rises over his head.[17] You have a figure of him in the British Museum. He is Infinite Time and Long Duration; he is the supreme god of the Mithraic hierarchy and creates and destroys all things, the durée créatrice of Bergson. He is a sun-god. Leo is the zodiacal sign where the sun dwells in summer, while the snake symbolizes the winter or wet time. So Aion, the lion-headed god with the snake round his body, again represents the union of opposites, light and darkness, male and female, creation and destruction. The god is represented as having his arms crossed and holding a key in each hand. He is the spiritual father of St Peter, for he too holds the keys. The keys which Aion is holding are the keys to the past and future.

The ancient mystery cults are always connected with psycho-pompic deities. Some of these deities are equipped with the keys to the underworld, because as the guardians of the door they watch over the descent of the initiates into the darkness and are the leaders into the mysteries. Hecate is one of them.

In our dream the key is the key to the city of Toledo, so we have to consider the symbolic meaning of Toledo and of the city. As the old capital of Spain, Toledo was a very strong fortification and the very ideal of a feudal city, a refuge and stronghold which could not easily be touched from outside. The city represents a totality, closed in upon itself, a power which cannot be destroyed, which has existed for centuries and will exist for many centuries more. Therefore the city symbolizes the totality of man, an attitude of wholeness which cannot be dissolved.

The city as a synonym for the self, for psychic totality, is an old and well-known image. We read for instance in the Oxyrhynchus sayings of Jesus:[13] 'A city built up on the top of a high hill and stablished, can neither fall nor be hid'. And: 'Strive therefore to know yourselves, and ye shall be aware that ye are the sons of the almighty Father; and ye shall know that ye are in the city of God and ye are the city'. There is a Coptic treatise in the Codex Brucianus in which we find the idea of the Monogenes or only son of God, who is also the Anthropos, Man.[14] He is called the city with the four gates. The city with the four gates symbolizes the idea of totality; it is the individual who possesses the four gates to the world, the four psychological functions, and so is contained in the self. The city with the four gates is his indestructible wholeness – consciousness and the unconscious united.

So these depths, that layer of utter unconsciousness in our dream, contain at the same time the key to individual completeness and wholeness, in other words to healing. The meaning of 'whole' or 'wholeness' is to make holy or to heal. The descent into the depths will bring healing. It is the way to the total being, to the treasure which suffering mankind is forever seeking, which is hidden in the place guarded by terrible danger. This is the place of primordial unconsciousness and at the same time the place of healing and redemption, because it contains the jewel of wholeness. It is the cave where the dragon of chaos lives and it is also the indestructible city, the magic circle or *temenos*, the sacred precinct where all the split-off parts of the personality are united.

The use of a magic circle or mandala, as it is called in the East, for healing purposes is an archetypal idea. When a man is ill the Pueblo Indians of New Mexico make a sand-painting of a mandala with four gates. In the centre of it they build the so-called sweat-house or medicine-lodge, where the patient has to undergo the sweat-cure. On the floor of the medicine-lodge is painted another magic circle – being thus placed in the centre of the big mandala – and in the midst of it is the bowl with the healing water. The water symbolizes the entrance to the underworld. The healing process in this ceremony is clearly analogous to the symbolism which we find in the collective unconscious. It is an individuation process, an identification with the totality of the personality, with the self. In Christian symbolism the totality is Christ, and the healing process consists of the *imitatio Christi*. The four gates are replaced by the arms of the cross.

The serpent in the cave in our dream is the friend of B— C—, the hero of the dreamer's early days, into whom he projected everything he wanted to become and all the virtues to which he was aspiring. That young friend is at peace with the serpent. He is a child without guile, he is innocent and knows as yet of no conflict. Therefore he has the key to Spain and the power over the four gates.[15]

DISCUSSION

Dr David Yellowlees:

I need hardly mention that I shall not attempt to discuss anything that has been said tonight. We are all glad Professor Jung has given us such an extraordinarily fascinating account of his own views, rather than spend time on controversial matters. But I think some of us would be grateful if he would recognize that we approach psychology and psychotherapy along lines not exclusively Freudian perhaps, but in accordance with certain fundamental principles with which Freud's name is associated, though he may not have originated them. We are very grateful that Professor Jung has given us what we believe to be a wider view. Some of us prefer that view, and perhaps the

Freudians would be able to tell us why. But the question was raised the other night as to the relationship between the concept of the unconscious which Professor Jung has been laying before us and Freud's concept of it, and I think if Professor Jung will be so good he could help us a little in that direction. I know quite well I may be misinterpreting him, but the impression I got on Tuesday night was almost as if he had said that he was dealing with facts and Freud with theories. He knows as well as I do that this bald statement really requires some amplification and I wish he could tell us, for example, what we ought to do from a therapeutic point of view when faced with a patient who produces spontaneously what I would call Freudian material, and how far we should regard Freudian theories simply as theories in view of the evidence which can be proved by such material as infantile fixation of the libido – oral, anal, phallic, and so on. If Professor Jung would say a little to give us some kind of correlation we would be very grateful.

Professor Jung:

I told you at the beginning that I do not want to be critical. I just want to give you a point of view of my own, of how I envisage psychological material, and I suppose that when you have heard what I have to contribute you will be able to make up your minds about these questions, and how much of Freud, how much of Adler, or myself, or I do not know whom, you will want to follow. If you want me to elucidate the question of the connection with Freud, I am quite glad to do it. I started out entirely on Freud's lines. I was even considered to be his best disciple. I was on excellent terms with him until I had the idea that certain things are symbolical. Freud would not agree to this, and he identified his method with the theory and the theory with the method. That is impossible, you cannot identify a method with science. I said that in view of these things I could not keep on publishing the *Jahrbuch*[16] and I withdrew.

But I am perfectly well aware of the merits of Freud and I do not want to diminish them. I know that what Freud says agrees with many people, and I assume that these people have exactly the kind of psychology that he describes. Adler, who has entirely different views, also has a large following, and I am convinced that many people have an Adlerian psychology. I too have a following – not so large as Freud's – and it consists presumably of people who have my psychology. I consider my contribution to psychology to be my subjective confession. It is my personal psychology, my prejudice that I see psychological facts as I do. I admit that I see things in such and such a way. But I expect Freud and Adler to do the same and confess that their ideas are their subjective point of view. So far as we admit our personal prejudice, we are really contributing towards an objective psychology. We cannot help being prejudiced by our ancestors, who want to look at things in a certain way, and so we instinctively have certain points of view. I would be neurotic if I saw things in another way than my instinct tells me to do; my snake, as the primitives say, would be all against me. When Freud said certain things, my snake did not agree. And I take the route that my snake prescribes, because that is good for me. But I have patients with whom I have to make a Freudian analysis and go into all the details which Freud has correctly described. I have other cases that force me to an Adlerian point of view, because they have a power complex. People who have the capacity to adapt and are successful are more inclined to have a Freudian psychology, because a man in that position is looking for the gratification of his desires, while the man who has not been successful has no time to think about desires. He has only one desire – to succeed, and he will have an Adlerian psychology, because a man who always falls into the second place will develop a power complex.

I have no power complex in that sense because I have been fairly successful and in nearly every respect I have been able to adapt. If the whole world disagrees with me it is perfectly indifferent to me. I have a perfectly good place in Switzerland, I enjoy myself, and if nobody enjoys my books I enjoy them. I know nothing better than being in my library, and if I make discoveries in my books, that is wonderful. I cannot say I have a Freudian psychology because I never had such difficulties in relation to desires. As a boy I lived in the country and took things very naturally, and the natural and unnatural things of which Freud speaks were not interesting to me. To talk of an incest complex just bores me to tears. But I know exactly how I could make myself neurotic: if I said or believed something that is not myself. I say what I see, and if somebody agrees with me it pleases me and if nobody agrees it is indifferent to me. I can join neither the Adlerian nor the Freudian confession. I can agree only with the Jungian confession because I see things that way even if there is not a single person on earth who shares my views. The only thing I hope for is to give you some interesting ideas and let you see how I tackle things.

It is always interesting to me to see a craftsman at work. His skill makes the charm of a craft. Psychotherapy is a craft and I deal in my individual way – a very humble way with nothing particular to show – with the things I have to do. Not that I believe for a moment that I am absolutely right. Nobody is absolutely right in psychological matters. Never forget that in psychology the *means* by which you judge and observe the psyche is the *psyche* itself. Have you ever heard of a hammer beating itself? In psychology the observer is the observed. The psyche is not only the *object* but also the *subject* of our science. So you see, it is a vicious circle and we have to be very modest. The best we can expect in psychology is that everybody puts his cards on the table and admits: 'I handle things in such and such a way, and this is how I see them'. Then we can compare notes.

I have always compared notes with Freud and Adler. Three books have been written by pupils of mine who tried to give a synopsis of the three points of view.[17] You have never heard this from the other side. That is our Swiss temperament. We are liberal and we try to see things side by side, together. From my point of view the best thing is to say that obviously there are thousands of people who have a Freudian psychology and thousands who have an Adlerian psychology. Some seek gratification of desire and some others fulfilment of power and yet others want to see the world as it is and leave things in peace. We do not want to change anything. The world is good as it is.

There are many different psychologies in existence. A certain American university, year after year, issues a volume of the psychologies of 1934, 1935, and so on. There is a total chaos in psychology, so do not be so frightfully serious about psychological theories. Psychology is not a religious creed but a point of view, and when we are human about it we may be able to understand each other. I admit that some people have sexual trouble and others have other troubles. I have chiefly other troubles. You now have an idea of how I look at things. My problem is to wrestle with the big monster of the historical past, the great snake of the centuries, the burden of the human mind, the problem of Christianity. It would be so much simpler if I knew nothing; but I know too much, through my ancestors and my own education. Other people are not worried by such problems, they do not care about the historical burdens Christianity has heaped upon us. But there are people who are concerned with the great battle between the present and the past or the future. It is a tremendous human problem. Certain people make history and others build a little house in the suburbs. Mussolini's case is not settled by saying he has a power complex. He is concerned with politics, and that is his life and death. The world is huge and there is not one theory only to explain everything.

To Freud the unconscious is chiefly a receptacle for things repressed. He looks at it from the corner of the nursery. To me it is a vast historical storehouse. I acknowledge I have a nursery too, but it is small in comparison with the vast spaces of history which were more interesting to me from childhood than the nursery. There are many people like myself, I am optimistic in that respect. Once I thought there were no people like myself; I was afraid it was megalomania to think as I did. Then I found many people who fitted in with my point of view, and I was satisfied that I represented perhaps a minority of people whose basic psychological facts are expressed more or less happily by my formulation, and when you get these people under analysis you will find they do not agree with Freud's or Adler's point of view, but with mine. I have been reproached for my naïveté. When I am not sure about a patient I give him books by Freud and Adler and say, 'Make your choice', in the hope that we are going on the right track. Sometimes we are on the wrong track. As a rule, people who have reached a certain maturity and who are philosophically minded and fairly successful in the world and not too neurotic, agree with my point of view. But you must not conclude from what I present to you that I always lay my cards on the table and tell the patient all I mention here. Time would not allow me to go into all those details of interpretation. But a few cases need to acquire a great amount of knowledge and are grateful when they see a way to enlarge their point of view.

I cannot say where I could find common ground with Freud when he calls a certain part of the unconscious the Id. Why give it such a funny name? It is the unconscious and that is something we do not know. Why call it the Id? Of course the difference of temperament produces a different outlook. I never could bring myself to be so frightfully interested in these sex cases. They do exist, there are people with a neurotic sex life and you have to talk sex stuff with them until they get sick of it and you get out of that boredom. Naturally, with my temperamental attitude, I hope to goodness we shall get through with the stuff as quickly as possible. It is neurotic stuff and no reasonable normal person talks of it for any length of time. It is not natural to dwell on such matters. Primitives are very reticent about them. They allude to sexual intercourse by a word that is equivalent to 'hush'. Sexual things are taboo to them, as they really are to us if we are natural. But taboo things and places are always apt to be the receptacle for all sorts of projections. And so very often the real problem is not to be found there at all. Many people make unnecessary difficulties about sex when their actual troubles are of quite a different nature.

Once a young man came to me with a compulsion neurosis. He brought me a manuscript of his of a hundred and forty pages, giving a complete Freudian analysis of his case. It was quite perfect according to the rules, it could have been published in the *Jahrbuch*. He said: 'Will you read this and tell me why I am not cured although I made a complete psychoanalysis?' I said: 'So you have, and I do not understand it either. You ought to be cured according to all the rules of the art, but when you say you are not cured I have to believe you'. He repeated: 'Why am I not cured, having a complete insight into the structure of my neurosis?' I said: 'I cannot criticize your thesis. The whole thing is marvellously well demonstrated. There remains only one, perhaps quite foolish, question: you do not mention where you come from and who your parents are. You say you spent last winter on the Riviera and the summer in St Moritz. Were you very careful in the choice of your parents?' 'Not at all'. 'You have an excellent business and are making a good deal of money?' 'No, I cannot make money'. 'Then you have a big fortune from an uncle?' 'No'. 'Then where does the money come from?' He replied: 'I have a certain arrangement. I have a friend who gives me the money'. I said: 'It must be a wonderful friend', and he replied, 'It is a woman'. She was much older than himself, aged thirty-six, a teacher in an elementary school with a small salary, who, as an elderly spinster, fell in love with the fellow who was twenty-eight. She lived on bread and milk so that he could spend his winter on the Riviera and his summer in St Moritz. I said: 'And you ask why you are ill!' He said: 'Oh, you have a moralistic point of view; that is not scientific'. I said: 'The money in your pocket is the money of the woman you cheat'. He said, 'No, we agreed upon it. I had a serious talk with her and it is not a matter for discussion that I get the money from her'. I said: 'You are pretending to yourself that it is not her money, but you live by it, and that is immoral. That is the cause of your compulsion neurosis. It is a compensation and a punishment for an immoral attitude'. An utterly unscientific point of view, of course, but it is my conviction that he deserves his compulsion neurosis and will have it to the last day of his life if he behaves like a pig.

Dr T. A. Ross:

Did not that come out in the analysis?

Professor Jung:

He went right away like a god and thought: 'Dr Jung is only a moralist, not a scientist. Anybody else would have been impressed by the interesting case instead of looking for simple things'. He commits a crime and steals the savings of a lifetime from an honest woman in order to be able to have a good time. That fellow belongs in gaol, and his compulsion neurosis provides it for him all right.

Dr P. W. L. Camps:

I am a humble general practitioner, not a psychologist, and may be labelled as a suburban villa. I am an outsider in this place. The first night I thought I had no right to be here; the second night I was here again; the third night I was glad to be here; and the fourth night I am in a maze of mythology.

I would like to ask something about last night. We were sent away with the idea that perfection was most undesirable and completion the end and aim of existence. I slept soundly last night but I felt that I had had an ethical shock. Perhaps I am not gifted with much intellect and it was an intellectual shock too. Professor Jung declares himself a determinist or fatalist. After he had analysed a young man who went away disappointed and then went to bits, Professor Jung felt it was only right that he should go to bits. You as psychologists, I take it, are endeavouring to cure people, and you have a purpose in life, not merely to enjoy your interests, whether it be mythology or the study of human nature. You want to get at the bottom of human nature and try to build it up to something better.

I listened with the greatest interest to Professor Jung's simple English terms and rejoiced in them. I have been confounded with all this new terminology. To hear of our sensation and thinking and feeling and intuition – to which possibly an X may be added for something else – was most illuminating to me as an ordinary individual.

But I feel that we did not hear where the conscious or rather where the unconscious of the child develops. I fear that we did not hear enough about children. I should like to ask Professor Jung where the unconscious in the child does become the conscious.

I should also like to know whether we are not misled somewhat by this multitude of diagrams, barriers, Egos, and Ids, and other things I have seen portrayed; whether we could not improve on these diagrams by having a gradation of stages.

As Professor Jung has pointed out, we have inherited faces and eyes and ears and there are a multitude of faces and in psychology there are a multitude of types also. Is it not reasonable to suppose that there is an enormous possibility of varieties planted on that inheritance, that they are a sort of mesh, a sieve as it were, that will receive impressions and select them in the unconscious years of early life and reach through into consciousness later? I should like to ask Professor Jung whether these thoughts have crossed the mind of an eminent psychologist such as he is – the very greatest psychologist in my view – tonight?

Professor Jung:

After that severe reproach for immorality I owe an explanation of my cynical remarks of yesterday. I am not as bad as all that. I naturally try to do my best for my patients, but in psychology it is very important that the doctor should not strive to heal at all costs. One has to be exceedingly careful not to impose one's own will and conviction on the patient. We have to give him a certain amount of freedom. You can't wrest people away from their fate, just as in medicine you cannot cure a patient if nature means him to die. Sometimes it is really a question whether you are allowed to rescue a man from the fate he must undergo for the sake of his further development. You cannot save certain people from committing terrible nonsense because it is in their grain. If I take it away they have no merit. We only gain merit and psychological development by accepting ourselves as we are and by being serious enough to live the lives we are trusted with. Our sins and errors and mistakes are necessary to us, otherwise we are deprived of the most precious incentives to development. When a man goes away, having heard something which might have changed his mind, and does not pay attention, I do not call him back. You may accuse me of being unchristian, but I do not care. I am on the side of nature. The old Chinese Book of Wisdom says: 'The Master says it once'. He does not run after people, it is no good. Those who are meant to hear will understand, and those who are not meant to understand will not hear.

I was under the impression that my audience consisted chiefly of psychotherapists. If I had known that medical men were present I would have expressed myself more civilly. But psychotherapists will understand. Freud – to quote the master's own words – says it is not good to try to cure at all costs. He often repeated that to me, and he is right.

Psychological truths are two-edged, and whatever I say can be used in such a way that it can work the greatest evil, the greatest devastation and nonsense. There is not one statement I have made which has not been twisted into its opposite. So I do not insist on any statement. You can take it, but if you do not take it, all right. You may perhaps blame me for that, but I trust that there is a will to live in everybody which will help them to choose the thing that is right for them. When I am treating a man I must be exceedingly careful not to knock him down with my views or my personality, because he has to fight his lonely fight through life and he must be able to trust in his perhaps very incomplete armour and in his own perhaps very imperfect aim. When I say, 'That is not good and should be better', I deprive him of courage. He must plough his field with a plough that is not good perhaps; mine may be better, but what good is it to him? He has not got my plough, I have it and he cannot borrow it; he must use his own perhaps very incomplete tools and has to work with his own inherited capacities, whatever they are. I help him of course, I may say for instance: 'Your thinking is perfectly good, but perhaps in another respect you could improve'. If he does not want to hear it, I shall not insist because I do not want to make him deviate.

Dr Marion Mackenzie:

In the same way that the rich young man was not called back but went away sorrowful?

Professor Jung:

Yes, it is the same technique. If I were to say to a man, 'You should not go away', he would never come back. I have to say, 'Have your own way'. Then he will trust me.

As to the question about children, there has been in the last decades such a noise about children that I often scratch my head at a meeting and say: 'Are they all midwives and nurses?' Does not the world consist chiefly of parents and grandparents? The adults have the problems. Leave the poor children alone. I get the mother by the ears and not the child. The parents make the neuroses of children.

It is certainly interesting to make researches into the development of consciousness. The beginning of consciousness is a fluid condition, and you cannot say when the child has become really conscious and when it has not yet. But that belongs to an entirely different chapter: the psychology of the ages. There is a psychology of childhood, which apparently consists in the psychology of the respective parents; a psychology from infancy to puberty; a psychology of puberty; of the young man, of the adult man of thirty-five, of the man in the second half of life, of the man in old age. That is a science in itself, and I could not possibly bring in all that too. I have a most difficult time as it is to illustrate one single dream. Science is large. It is as if you expected a physicist, when he talks of the theory of light, to elucidate at the same time the whole of mechanical physics. It is simply not possible. Psychology is not an introductory course for nurses; it is a very serious science and consists of a heap of knowledge, so you should not expect too much from me. I am doing my level best to grapple with dreams and to tell you something about them, and I naturally cannot fulfil all expectations.

As to the question about perfection: to strive for perfection is a high ideal. But I say: 'Fulfil something you are able to fulfil rather than run after what you will never achieve'. Nobody is perfect. Remember the saying: 'None is good but God alone',[18] and nobody can be. It is an illusion. We can modestly strive to fulfil ourselves and to be as complete human beings as possible, and that will give us trouble enough.

Dr Eric B. Strauss:

Does Professor Jung intend to publish the reasons which led him to identify certain archetypal symbols with physiological processes?

Professor Jung:

The case you refer to was submitted to me by Dr Davie, and afterwards he published it without my knowledge.[19] I do not wish to say more about this correlation because I do not yet feel on very safe ground. Questions of differential diagnosis between organic disease and psychological symbols are very difficult, and I prefer not to say anything about it for the time being.

Dr Strauss:

But your diagnosis was made from the facts of the dream?

Professor Jung:

Yes, because the organic trouble disturbed the mental functioning. There was a serious depression and presumably a profound disturbance of the sympathetic system.

Dr H. Crichton-Miller:

Tomorrow is the last seminar, and there is a point that interests us that has not been referred to. That is the difficult problem of transference. I wonder if Professor Jung would think it proper to give us his view tomorrow – without dealing necessarily with other schools – as to transference and the proper handling of it?

NOTES

1   'And Isis, the great lady of enchantments, said, "Flow on, poison, and come forth from Rā. . . . I have worked, and I make the poison to fall on the ground, for the venom hath been mastered. . . . Let Rā live, and let the poison die; and if the poison live then Rā shall die". And similarly, a certain man, the son of a certain man, shall live, and the poison shall die'. E. A. Wallis Budge, *Egyptian Literature*, I, p. 55.

2   [*Symbols of Transformation*, pars. 375ff.]

3   R. Campbell Thompson, *The Epic of Gilgamish*.

4   [Josephus, *The Jewish War* 2.111–115.]

5   [Cf. *The Structure and Dynamics of the Psyche* (C.W., vol. 8), frontispiece and refs. with it.]

6   [Thus far, the dream is documented in the 'Life of Sophocles', sec. 12, in *Sophoclis Fabulae*, ed. Pearson, p. xix.]

7   [The people of ancient Phocaea, on the western coast of Asia Minor, founded Massilia (Marseilles) and colonies on the east coast of Spain.]

8   [Cf. *Psychological Types*, ch.V, 4a.]

9   [*Symbols of Transformation*, pars. 572f.]

10 [Cf. *Psychology and Alchemy*, par. 105, n. 35, citing Foucart, *Les Mystères d'Eleusis*. According to classicists, Asterios' report referred to rituals of Demeter celebrated at Alexandria in which a priest (not of Apollo) and a priestess performed the *hierosgamos*. The narration of *aischrologia* to please Demeter occurred during the Thesmophoria, an autumn festival in her honour, the Stenia, celebrating her return, and the mid-winter Haloa, sacred to her and Dionysus. Cf. Harrison, *Prolegomena*, ch. IV, esp. pp. 136, 148f.]

11 [Herodotus 2.60 (Penguin edn., pp. 125f.).]

12 [See *Aion* (C.W., vol. 9, ii), frontispiece, and *Symbols of Transformation*, index, s.v.]

13 [*New Sayings of Jesus and Fragment of a Lost Gospel*, ed. by Grenfell and Hunt, pp. 36 and 15.]

14 [It is MS. Bruce 96, Bodleian Library, Oxford. Cf. *Psychology and Alchemy*, par. 138f.]

15 [For further analysis of this dream, from the Basel Seminar (supra, p. vii), see Jung's *L'Homme à la découverte de son âme*, pp. 314 ff.]

16 [*Jahrbuch für psychoanalytische und psychopathologische Forschungen* (Leipzig and Vienna), the organ of the psychoanalytical movement. Jung withdrew from the editorship in 1913.]

17 W. M. Kranefeldt, *Secret Ways of the Mind*; G. R. Heyer, *The Organism of the Mind*; Gerhard Adler, *Entdeckung der Seele*.
18 [Luke 18:19.]
19 [See supra, p. 56, n. 15.]

LECTURE FIVE

The Chairman (Dr J. R. Rees):

Ladies and Gentlemen: You will have noticed that the Chairman's remarks have been growing shorter each evening. Yesterday Professor Jung was in the middle of a continuous story, and I think we all want him to get on with it straight away.

Professor Jung:

Ladies and Gentlemen: You remember that I began to give you the material belonging to this dream. I am now in the middle of it and there is a great more to come. But at the end of yesterday's lecture I was asked by Dr Crichton-Miller to speak about the problem of transference. That showed me something which seems to be of practical interest. When I analyse such a dream carefully and put in a great deal of work, it often happens that my colleagues wonder why I am heaping up such a quantity of learned material. They think, 'Well, yes, it shows his zeal and his goodwill to make something of a dream. But what is the practical use of all these parallels?'

I do not mind these doubts in the least. But I was really just about to bring in something belonging to the problem, and Dr Crichton-Miller has caught me in this attempt and asked just that question which any practical doctor would ask. Practical doctors are troubled by practical problems, and not by theoretical questions; therefore they always get a bit impatient when it comes to theoretical elucidations. They are particularly troubled by the half-amusing, half-painful, even tragic problems of transference. If you had been a little bit more patient, you would have seen that I was handling the very material by which transference can be analysed. But since the question has been raised I think I should rather give way to your wish and talk about the psychology and treatment of transference. But the choice is up to you. My feeling was that Dr Crichton-Miller had spoken the mind of the majority of you. Am I right in this assumption?

Members:

Yes.

Professor Jung:

I think you are right in your decision, for if I am going to speak about transference I shall have the opportunity to lead back to what I had originally intended with the analysis of that dream. I am afraid we will not have time to finish it; but I think it is better if I start from your actual problems and your actual difficulties.

I would never have been forced to work out that elaborate symbolism and this careful study of parallels if I had not been terribly worried by the problem of transference. So, in discussing the question of transference, an avenue will open to the kind of work I was trying to describe to you in my lecture last night. I told you in the beginning that my lectures will be a sorry torso. I am simply unable, in five evenings, even if I compress things together as I have done, to give you a complete summary of what I have to tell.

Speaking about the transference makes it necessary first to define the concept so that we really understand what we are talking about. You know that the word transference, originally coined by Freud, has become a sort of colloquial term; it has even found its way into the larger public. One generally means by it an awkward hanging-on, an adhesive sort of relationship.

The term 'transference' is the translation of the German word *Übertragung*. Literally *Übertragung* means: to carry something over from one place to another. The word *Übertragung* is also used in a metaphorical sense to designate the carrying over from one form into another. Therefore in German it is synonymous with *Übersetzung* – that is, translation.

The psychological process of transference is a specific form of the more general process of projection. It is important to bring these two concepts together and to realize that transference is a special case of projection – at least that is how I understand it. Of course, everybody is free to use the term in his own way.

Projection is a general psychological mechanism that carries over subjective contents of any kind into the object. For instance, when I say, 'The colour of this room is yellow', that is a projection, because in the object itself there is no yellow; yellow is only in us. Colour is our subjective experience as you know. The same when I hear a sound, that is a projection, because sound does not exist in itself; it is a sound in my head, it is a psychic phenomenon which I project.

Transference is usually a process that happens between two people and not between a human subject and a physical object, though there are exceptions; whereas the more general mechanism of projection, as we have seen, can just as well extend to physical objects. The mechanism of projection, whereby subjective contents are carried over into the object and appear as if belonging to it, is never a voluntary act, and transference, as a specific form of projection, is no exception to this rule. You cannot consciously and intentionally project, because then you know all the time that you are projecting your subjective contents; therefore you cannot locate them in the object, for you know that they really belong to you. In projection the apparent fact you are confronted with in the object is in reality an illusion; but you assume what you observe in the object not to be subjective, but objectively existing. Therefore, a projection is abolished when you find out that the apparently objective facts are really subjective contents. Then these contents become associated with your own psychology, and you cannot attribute them to the object any more.

Sometimes one is apparently quite aware of one's projections though one does not know their full extent. And that portion of which one is not aware remains unconscious and still appears as if belonging to the object. This often happens in practical analysis. You say, for instance: 'Now, look here, you simply project the image of your father into that man, or into myself', and you assume that this is a perfectly satisfactory explanation and quite sufficient to dissolve the projection. It is satisfactory to the doctor, perhaps, but not to the patient. Because, if there is still something more in that projection, the patient will keep on projecting. It does not depend upon his will; it is simply a phenomenon that produces itself. Projection is an automatic, spontaneous fact. It is simply there; you do not know how it happens. You just find it there. And this rule, which holds good for projection in general, is also true of transference. Transference is something which is just there. If it exists at all, it is there *a priori*. Projection is always an *unconscious* mechanism, therefore consciousness, or conscious realization, destroys it.

Transference, strictly, as I have already said, is a projection which happens between two individuals and which, as a rule, is of an emotional and compulsory nature. Emotions in themselves are always in some degree overwhelming for the subject, because they are involuntary conditions which override the intentions of the ego. Moreover, they cling to the subject, and he cannot detach them from himself. Yet this involuntary condition of the subject is at the same time projected into the object, and through that a bond is established which cannot be broken, and exercises a compulsory influence upon the subject.

Emotions are not detachable like ideas or thoughts, because they are identical with certain physical conditions and are thus deeply rooted in the heavy matter of the body. Therefore the emotion of the projected contents always forms a link, a sort of dynamic relationship, between the subject and the object – and that is the transference. Naturally, this emotional link or bridge or elastic string can be positive or negative, as you know.

The projection of emotional contents always has a peculiar influence. Emotions are contagious, because they are deeply rooted in the sympathetic system; hence the word 'sympathicus'. Any process of an emotional kind immediately arouses similar processes in others. When you are in a crowd which is moved by an emotion, you cannot fail to be roused by that same emotion. Suppose you are in a country where a language is spoken which you don't understand, and somebody makes a joke and people laugh, then you laugh too in an idiotic way, simply because you can't refrain from laughing. Also when you are in a crowd which is politically excited you can't help being excited too, even when you do not share their opinion at all, because emotion has this suggestive effect. The French psychologists have dealt with this 'contagion mentale'; there are some very good books on the subject, especially The Crowd: A Study of the Popular Mind, by Le Bon.

In psychotherapy, even if the doctor is entirely detached from the emotional contents of the patient, the very fact that the patient has emotions has an effect upon him. And it is a great mistake if the doctor thinks he can lift himself out of it. He cannot do more than become conscious of the fact that he is affected. If he does not see that, he is too aloof and then he talks beside the point. It is even his duty to accept the emotions of the patient and to mirror them. That is the reason why I reject the idea of putting the patient upon a sofa and sitting behind him. I put my patients in front of me and I talk to them as one natural human being to another, and I expose myself completely and react with no restriction.

I remember very well a case of an elderly woman of about fifty-eight – a doctor too – from the United States. She arrived in Zurich in a state of utter bewilderment. She was so confused at first I thought her half crazy, until I discovered that she had been in an analysis. She told me certain things she had done in her bewilderment, and it was quite obvious that she would never have done these things if her analyst had been a human being and not a mystical cipher who was sitting behind her, occasionally saying a wise word out of the clouds and never showing an emotion. So she got quite lost in her own mists and did some foolish things which he could easily have prevented her from doing if he had behaved like a human being. When she told me all that, I naturally had an emotional reaction and swore, or something like that. Upon which she shot out of her chair and said reproachfully, 'But you have an emotion!' I answered, 'Why, of course I have an emotion'. She said, 'But you should not have an emotion'. I replied, 'Why not? I have a good right to an emotion'. She objected, 'But you are an analyst!' I said, 'Yes, I am an analyst, and I have emotions. Do you think that I am an idiot or a catatonic?' 'But analysts have no emotions'. I remarked, 'Well, your analyst apparently had no emotions, and, if I may say so, he was a fool!' That one moment cleared her up completely; she was absolutely different from then on. She said, 'Thank heaven! Now I know where I am. I know there is a human being opposite me who has human emotions!' My emotional reaction had given her orientation. She wasn't a thinking type, she was a feeling type and therefore needed that kind of orientation. But her analyst was a man who simply thought and existed in his intellect, and had no connection with her feeling-life. She was a highly emotional sanguine sort of person who needed the emotionality and the feeling gesture of another human being in order not to feel alone. When you have to treat a feeling type and you talk intellectual stuff exclusively it is the same as if you, as the only intellectual, were talking to a company of feeling types. You would be utterly lost; you would feel as if you were at the North Pole, because you wouldn't be understood; nobody would react to your ideas. People would all be frightfully nice – and you would feel utterly foolish because they would not respond to your way of thinking.

One always has to answer people in their main function, otherwise no contact is established. So, in order to be able to show my patients that their reactions have arrived in my system, I have to sit opposite them so that they can read the reactions in my face and can see that I am listening. If I sit behind them, then I can yawn, I can sleep, I can go off on my own thoughts, and I can do what I please. They never know what is happening to me, and then they remain in an auto-erotic and isolated condition which is not good for ordinary people. Of course, if they were going to prepare for an existence as hermits on the Himalayas, it would be a different matter.

The emotions of patients are always slightly contagious, and they are very contagious when the contents which the patient projects into the analyst are identical with the analyst's own unconscious contents. Then they both fall into the same dark hole of unconsciousness, and get into the condition of participation. This is the phenomenon which Freud has described as counter-transference. It consists of mutual projecting into each other and being fastened together by mutual unconsciousness. Participation, as I have told you, is a characteristic of primitive psychology, that is, of a psychological level where there is no conscious discrimination between subject and object. Mutual unconsciousness is of course most confusing both to the analyst and to the patient; all orientation is lost, and the end of such an analysis is disaster.

Even analysts are not absolutely perfect, and it can happen that they are occasionally unconscious in certain respects. Therefore long ago I stipulated that analysts ought to be analysed themselves; they should have a father confessor or a mother confessor. Even the Pope, for all his infallibility, has to confess regularly, and not to a monsignor or a cardinal but to an ordinary priest. If the analyst does not keep in touch with his unconscious objectively, there is no guarantee whatever that the patient will not fall into the unconscious of the analyst. You probably all know certain patients who possess a diabolical cunning in finding out the weak spot, the vulnerable place in the analyst's psyche. To that spot they seek to attach the projections of their own unconscious. One usually says that it is a characteristic of women, but that is not true, men do just the same. They always find out this vulnerable spot in the analyst, and he can be sure that, whenever something gets into him, it will be exactly in that place where he is without defence. That is the place where he is unconscious himself and where he is apt to make exactly the same projections as the patient. Then the condition of participation happens, or, more strictly speaking, a condition of personal contamination through mutual unconsciousness.

One has, of course, all sorts of ideas about transference, and we are all somewhat prejudiced by the definition which Freud has given; one is inclined to think that it is always a matter of erotic transference. But my experience has not confirmed the theory that it is erotic contents or infantile things exclusively that are projected. According to my experience, anything can be a matter for projection, and the erotic transference is just one of the many possible forms of transference. There are many other contents in the human unconscious which are also of a highly emotional nature, and they can project themselves just as well as sexuality. All activated contents of the unconscious have the tendency to appear in projection. It is even the rule that an unconscious content which is constellated shows itself first as a projection. Any activated archetype can appear in projection, either into an external situation, or into people, or into circumstances – in short, into all sorts of objects. There are even transferences to animals and to things.

Not very long ago I had an interesting case of an unusually intelligent man. I explained to him a projection he had 'made'; he had projected his unconscious image of woman into a real woman, and the dreams showed very clearly just where the real person was utterly different from what he expected her to be. The fact went home. Then he said, 'If I had known that two years ago it would have saved me 40,000 francs!' I asked, 'How is that?' 'Well, somebody showed me an old Egyptian sculpture, and I instantly fell in love with it. It was an Egyptian cat, a very beautiful thing'. He instantly bought it for 40,000 francs and put it on the mantelpiece in his drawing-room. But then he found that he had lost his peace of mind. His office was on the floor below, and nearly every hour he had to jump up from his work to look at the cat, and when he had satisfied his desire he went back to work only to go upstairs again after some time. This restlessness became so disagreeable that he put the cat on his desk right opposite him – to find that he couldn't work any more! Then he had to lock it away in the attic in order to be liberated from its influence, and he had to fight down a continuous temptation to open the box and look at the cat again. When he understood his general projection of the feminine image – for, of course, the cat symbolized the woman – then the whole charm and fascination of the sculpture was gone.

That was a projection into a physical object, and it made the cat into a living being to whom he always had to return as some people return to the analyst. As you know, the analyst is often accused of having snake's eyes, of magnetizing or hypnotizing people, of forcing them to come back to him, of not letting them go. There *are* certain exceptionally bad cases of counter-transference when the analyst really cannot let go of the patient; but usually such accusations are the expression of a very disagreeable kind of projection which may even amount to ideas of persecution.

The intensity of the transference relationship is always equivalent to the importance of its contents to the subject. If it is a particularly intense transference, we can be sure that the contents of the projection, once they are extracted and made conscious, will prove to be just as important to the patient as the transference was. When a transference collapses it does not vanish into the air; its intensity, or a corresponding amount of energy, will appear in another place, for instance in another relationship, or in some other important psychological form. For the intensity of the transference is an intense emotion which is really the property of the patient. If the transference is dissolved, all that projected energy falls back into the subject, and he is then in possession of the treasure which formerly, in the transference, had simply been wasted.

Now we have to say a few words about the *aetiology* of the transference. Transference can be an entirely spontaneous and unprovoked reaction, a sort of 'love at first sight'. Of course transference should never be misunderstood as love; it has nothing to do with love whatever. Transference only misuses love. It may appear as if transference were love, and inexperienced analysts make the mistake of taking it for love, and the patient makes the same mistake and says that he is in love with the analyst. But he is not in love at all.

Occasionally a transference can even spring up before the first sight, that is before or outside the treatment. And if it happens to a person who does not come for analysis afterwards, we cannot find out the reasons. But this shows all the more that it has nothing whatever to do with the real personality of the analyst.

Once a lady came to me whom I had seen about three weeks before at a social reception. I had not even spoken to her then, I had only talked to her husband, and I knew him only rather superficially. The lady then wrote for a consultation, and I gave her an appointment. She came, and when she was at the door of my consulting room she said, 'I don't want to enter'. I replied, 'You don't have to enter; you can go away, of course! I have absolutely no interest in having you here if you don't want to come'. Then she said, 'But I must!' I answered, 'I'm not forcing you'. 'But you forced me to come'. 'How did I do that?' I thought she was crazy, but she was not crazy at all, she merely had a transference which pulled her to me. She had made some kind of projection in the meantime, and that projection had such a high emotional value for her that she could not resist it; she was magically drawn to come to me because that elastic string was too strong for her. In the course of her analysis we naturally found out what the contents of that non-provoked transference were.

Usually a transference establishes itself only during the analysis. Very often it is caused by a difficulty in making contact, in establishing emotional harmony between the doctor and the patient – what the French psychologists at the time of hypnotic and suggestion therapy used to call 'le rapport'. A good rapport means that the doctor and patient are getting on well together, that they can really talk to each other and that there is a certain amount of mutual confidence. Of course, at the time of the hypnotic therapists, the whole hypnotic and suggestive effect depended on the existence or non-existence of the rapport. In analytical treatment, if the rapport between analyst and patient is difficult on account of differences of personality, or if there are other psychological distances between them that hinder the therapeutic effect, that lack of contact causes the unconscious of the patient to try to cover the distance by building a compensatory bridge. Since there is no common ground, no possibility of forming any kind of relationship, a passionate feeling or an erotic fantasy attempts to fill the gap.

This often happens to people who habitually resist other human beings – either because of an inferiority complex or because of megalomania, or for other reasons – and who are psychologically very isolated. Then, out of fear of getting lost, their nature causes a violent effort of the emotions to attach themselves to the analyst. They are in despair that perhaps he too will not understand them; so they try to propitiate either the circumstances, or the analyst, or their own unwillingness by a sort of sexual attraction.

All these compensatory phenomena can be turned round and be applied to the analyst as well. Suppose, for instance, that an analyst has to treat a woman who does not particularly interest him, but suddenly he discovers that he has a sexual fantasy about her. Now I don't wish it on analysts that they should have such fantasies, but if they do they had better realize it, because it is important information from their unconscious that their human contact with the patient is not good, that there is a disturbance of rapport. Therefore the analyst's unconscious makes up for the lack of a decent human rapport by forcing a fantasy upon him in order to cover the distance and to build a bridge. These fantasies can be visual, they can be a certain feeling or a sensation – a sexual sensation, for instance. They are invariably a sign that the analyst's attitude to the patient is wrong, that he overvalues him or undervalues him or that he does not pay the right attention. That correction of his attitude can also be expressed by dreams. So if you dream of a patient, always pay attention and try to see whether the dream is showing you where you may be wrong. Patients are tremendously grateful when you are honest in that respect, and they feel it very much when you are dishonest or neglectful.

I once had a most instructive case of that sort. I was treating a young girl of about twenty or twenty-four. She had had a very peculiar childhood; she was born in Java of a very good European family, and had a native nurse.[1] As happens with children born in the colonies, the exotic environment and that strange and, in this case, even barbarous civilization got under her skin, and the whole emotional and instinctual life of the child became tainted with that peculiar atmosphere. That atmosphere is something the white man in the East hardly ever realizes; it is the psychic atmosphere of the native in regard to the white man, an atmosphere of intense fear – fear of the cruelty, the recklessness, and the tremendous and unaccountable power of the white man. That atmosphere infects children born in the East; the fear creeps into them and fills them with unconscious fantasies about the cruelty of the white man, and their psychology gets a peculiar twist and their sex life often goes completely wrong. They suffer from unaccountable nightmares and panics and cannot adapt themselves to normal circumstances when it comes to the problem of love and marriage and so on.

That was the case with this girl. She went hopelessly astray and got into the most risky erotic situations, and she acquired a very bad reputation. She adopted inferior ways; she began to paint and powder herself in a rather conspicuous fashion, also to wear big ornaments in order to satisfy the primitive woman in her blood, or rather in her skin, so that she could join in and help her to live. Because she could not and naturally would not live without her instincts, she had to do all sorts of things which went too low. For instance, she easily succumbed to bad taste; she wore terrible colours to please the primitive unconscious in her so that it would join in when she wanted to interest a man. But naturally her choice of men was also below the mark, and so she got into a frightful tangle. Her nickname was 'the great whore of Babylon'. All this was, of course, most unfortunate for an otherwise decent girl. When she came to me she really looked absolutely forbidding, so that I felt pretty awkward on account of my own maids when she was in my office for an hour. I said, 'Now, you simply can't look like that, you look like—' and I said something exceedingly drastic. She was very sad over it but she couldn't help it.

At this point I dreamed of her in the following way: *I was on a highway at the foot of a high hill, and upon the hill was a castle, and in that castle was a high tower, the donjon. On top of that high tower was a loggia, a beautiful open contrivance with pillars and a beautiful marble balustrade, and upon that balustrade sat an elegant figure of a woman. I looked up – and I had to look up so that I felt the pain in my neck even afterwards – and the figure was my patient!* Then I woke up and instantly I thought, 'Heavens! Why does my unconscious put that girl so high up?' And immediately the thought struck me, 'I have looked down on her'. For I really thought that she was bad. My dream showed me that this was a mistake, and I knew that I had been a bad doctor. So I told her the next day: 'I have had a dream about you where I had to look up to you so that my neck hurt me, and the reason for this compensation is that I have looked down on you'. That worked miracles, I can tell you! No trouble with the transference any more, because I simply got right with her and met her on the right level.

I could tell you quite a number of informative dreams like that about the doctor's own attitude. And when you really try to be on a level with the patient, not too high nor too low, when you have the right attitude, the right appreciation, then you have much less trouble with the transference. It won't save you from it entirely, but sure enough you won't have those bad forms of transference which are mere over-compensations for a lack of rapport.

There is another reason for over-compensation by transference in the case of patients with an utterly auto-erotic attitude; patients who are shut away in auto-erotic insulation and have a thick coat of armour, or a thick wall and moat around them. Yet they have a desperate need for human contact, and they naturally begin to crave for a human being outside the walls. But they don't do anything about it. They won't lift a finger, and neither will they allow anybody to approach them, and from this attitude they get a terrible transference. Such transferences cannot be touched, because the patients are too well defended on all sides. On the contrary, if you try to do something about the transference, they feel it as a sort of aggression, and they defend themselves still more. So you must leave these people to roast in their own fat until they are satisfied and come voluntarily out of their fortress. Of course they will complain like anything about your lack of understanding and so on, but the only thing you can do is to be patient and say, 'Well, you are inside, you show nothing, and as long as you don't show anything I can do nothing either'.

In such a case the transference can come almost to the boiling point, because only a strong flame will cause the person to leave his castle. Of course that means a great outburst; but the outburst must be borne quietly by the doctor, and the patient will later on be very thankful that he has not been taken literally. I remember the case of a colleague of mine – and I can safely tell you of this case because she is dead – an American woman who came to me under very complicated circumstances. In the beginning she was on her high horse. You know there are peculiar institutions in America called universities and colleges for women; in our technical language we call them animus incubators, and they turn out annually a large number of fearful persons. Now she was such a bird. She was 'very competent', and she had got into a disagreeable transference situation. She was an analyst and had a case of a married man who fell wildly in love with her, apparently. It was not, of course, love, it was transference. He projected into her that she wanted to marry him but would not admit that she was in love with him and so wasted no end of flowers and chocolates and finery over her, and finally he even threatened her with a revolver. So she had to leave at once and come to me.

It soon turned out that she had no idea of a woman's feeling-life. She was O.K. as a doctor, but whatever touched the sphere of a man was absolutely and utterly strange to her. She was even blissfully ignorant of a man's anatomy, because at the university where she had studied one only dissected female bodies. So you can imagine the situation with which I was confronted.

Naturally I saw it coming, and I saw right away why the man had fallen into the trap. She was totally unconscious of herself as a woman; she was just a man's mind with wings underneath, and the whole woman's body was non-existent, and her patient was forced by nature to fill the gap. He had to prove to her that a man does exist and that a man has a claim, that she was a woman and that she should respond to him. It was her female non-existence that baited the trap. He was, of course, equally unconscious, because he did not see at all that she did not exist as a woman. You see, he also was such a bird, consisting of only a head with wings underneath. He also was not a man. We often discover with Americans that they are tremendously unconscious of themselves. Sometimes they suddenly grow aware of themselves, and then you get these interesting stories of decent young girls eloping with Chinamen or with Negroes, because in the American that primitive layer, which with us is a bit difficult, with them is disagreeable, as it is much lower down. It is the same phenomenon as 'going black' or 'going native' in Africa.

Now these two people both came into this awful transference situation, and one could say they were both entirely crazy, and therefore the woman had to run away. The treatment was, of course, perfectly clear. One had to make her conscious of herself as a woman, and a woman never becomes conscious of herself as long as she cannot accept the fact of her feelings. Therefore her unconscious arranged a marvellous transference to me, which naturally she would not accept, and I did not force it upon her. She was just such a case of complete insulation, and facing her with her transference would merely have forced her into a position of defence which of course would have defeated the whole purpose of the treatment. So I never spoke of it and just let things go, and quietly worked along with the dreams. The dreams, as they always do, were steadily informing us of the progress of her transference. I saw the climax coming and knew that one day a sudden explosion would take place. Of course, it would be a bit disagreeable and of a very emotional nature, as you have perhaps noticed in your own experience, and I foresaw a highly sentimental situation. Well, you just have to put up with it; you cannot help it. After six months of very quiet and painstaking systematic work she couldn't hold herself in any longer, and suddenly she almost shouted: 'But I love you!' and then she broke down and fell upon her knees and made an awful mess of herself.

You just have to stand such a moment. It is really awful to be thirty-four years old and to discover suddenly that you are human. Then it comes, of course, as a big lump to you and that lump is often indigestible. If I had told her six months before that the moment would come when she would make declarations of love, she would have jumped off to the moon. Hers was a condition of auto-erotic insulation, and the rising flame, the increasing fire of her emotions finally burned through the walls, and naturally it all came out as a sort of organic eruption. She was the better for its happening, and in that moment even the transference situation in America was settled.

You probably think that all this sounds pretty cold-blooded. As a matter of fact, you can only cope decently with such a situation when you do not behave as if you were superior. You have to accompany the process and lower your consciousness and feel along the situation, in order not to differ too much from your patient; otherwise he feels too awkward and will have the most terrible resentment afterwards. So it is quite good to have a reserve of sentiments which you can allow to play on such an occasion. Of course it requires some experience and routine to strike the right note. It is not always quite easy, but one has to bridge over these painful moments so that the reactions of the patient will not be too bad.

I have already mentioned a further reason for the transference, and that is mutual unconsciousness and contamination.[2] The case which I just told you about provides an example of this. Contamination through mutual unconsciousness happens as a rule when the analyst has a similar lack of adaptation to that of the patient; in other words, when he is neurotic. In so far as the analyst is neurotic, whether his neurosis be good or bad, he has an open wound, somewhere there is an open door which he does not control, and there a patient will get in, and then the analyst will be contaminated. Therefore it is an important postulate that the analyst should know as much as possible about himself.

I remember the case of a young girl who had been with two analysts before she came to me, and when she came to me she had the identical dream she had had when she was with those analysts.[3] Each time at the very beginning of her analysis she had a particular dream: *She came to the frontier and she wanted to cross it, but she could not find the custom-house where she should have gone to declare whatever she carried with her.* In the first dream she was seeking the frontier, but she did not even come to it. That dream gave her the feeling that she would never be able to find the proper relation to her analyst; but because she had feelings of inferiority and did not trust her judgment, she remained with him, and nothing came of it at all. She worked with him for two months and then she left.

She then went to another analyst. Again she dreamed that *she came to the frontier; it was a black night, and the only thing she could see was a faint little light. Somebody said that that was the light in the custom-house, and she tried to get to it. On the way she went down a hill and crossed a valley. In the depths of the valley was a dark wood and she was afraid to go on, but nevertheless she went through it, and suddenly she felt that somebody was clinging to her in the darkness. She tried to shake herself free, but that somebody clung to her still more, and she suddenly discovered that it was her analyst.* Now what happened was that after about three months of work this analyst developed a violent counter-transference to her, which the initial dream had foreseen.

When she came to me – she had seen me before at a lecture and had made up her mind to work with me – she dreamed that *she was coming to the Swiss frontier. It was day and she saw the custom-house. She crossed the frontier and she went into the custom-house, and there stood a Swiss customs official. A woman went in front of her and he let that woman pass, and then her turn came. She had only a small bag with her, and she thought she would pass unnoticed. But the official looked at her and said: 'What have you got in your bag?' She said: 'Oh, nothing at all', and opened it. He put his hand in and pulled out something that grew bigger and bigger, until it was two complete beds.* Her problem was that she had a resistance against marriage; she was engaged and would not marry for certain reasons, and those beds were the marriage-beds. I pulled that complex out of her and made her realize the problem, and soon after she married.

These initial dreams are often most instructive. Therefore I always ask a new patient when he first comes to me: 'Did you know some time ago that you were coming? Have you met me before? Have you had a dream lately, perhaps last night?' – because if he did, it gives me most valuable information about his attitude. And when you keep in close touch with the unconscious you can turn many a difficult corner. A transference is always a hindrance; it is never an advantage. You cure in spite of the transference, not because of it.

Another reason for the transference, particularly for bad forms of it, is provocation on the part of the analyst. There are certain analysts, I am sorry to say, who work for a transference because they believe, I don't know why, that transference is a useful and even necessary part of the treatment; therefore patients *ought* to have a transference. Of course this is an entirely mistaken idea. I have often had cases who came to me after a previous analysis and who after a fortnight or so became almost desperate. So far things had gone on very nicely and I was fully confident that the case would work out beautifully – and suddenly the patients informed me that they could not go on, and then the tears came. I asked, 'Why can't you go on? Have you got no money, or what is the matter?' They said, 'Oh no, that is not the reason. I have no transference'. I said, 'Thank heaven you have no transference! A transference is an illness. It is abnormal to have a transference. Normal people never have transferences'. Then analysis goes on again quietly and nicely.

We do not need transference just as we do not need projection. Of course, people will have it nevertheless. They always have projections but not the kind they expect. They have read Freud on transference, or they have been with another analyst, and it has been pumped into them that they ought to have a transference or they will never be cured. This is perfect nonsense. Transference or no transference, that has nothing to do with the cure. It is simply due to a peculiar psychological condition that there are these projections, and, just as one dissolves other projections by making them conscious, one has to dissolve the transference by making it conscious too. If there is no transference, so much the better. You get the material just the same. It is not transference that enables the patient to bring out his material; you get all the material you could wish for from dreams. The dreams bring out everything that is necessary. If you work for a transference, most likely you will provoke one, and the result of the analysis will be bad; for you can only provoke a transference by insinuating the wrong things, by arousing expectations, by making promises in a veiled way, which you do not mean to keep because you could not. You cannot possibly have affairs with eleven thousand virgins, and so you cheat people. An analyst is not allowed to be too friendly, otherwise he will be caught by it; he will produce an effect which goes beyond him. He cannot pay the bill when it is presented, and he should not provoke something for which he is not willing to pay. Even if the analyst means to do it for the good of the patient, it is a very misguided way, and it is always a great mistake. Leave people where they are. It does not matter whether they love the analyst or not. We are not all Germans who want to be loved when they sell you a pair of sock-suspenders. It is too sentimental. The patient's main problem is precisely to learn how to live his own life, and you don't help him when you meddle with it.

Those are some of the reasons for a transference. The general psychological reason for projection is always an activated unconscious that seeks expression. The intensity of the transference is equivalent to the importance of the projected content. A strong transference of a violent nature corresponds to a fiery content; it contains something important, something of great value to the patient. But as long as it is projected, the analyst seems to embody this most precious and important thing. He can't help being in this unfortunate position, but he has to give that value back to the patient, and the analysis is not finished until the patient has integrated the treasure. So, if a patient projects the saviour complex into you, for instance, you have to give back to him nothing less than a saviour – whatever that means. But you are not the saviour – most certainly not.

Projections of an archetypal nature involve a particular difficulty for the analyst. Each profession carries its respective difficulties, and the danger of analysis is that of becoming infected by transference projections, in particular by archetypal contents. When the patient assumes that his analyst is the fulfilment of his dreams, that he is not an ordinary doctor but a spiritual hero and a sort of saviour, of course the analyst will say, 'What nonsense! This is just morbid. It is a hysterical exaggeration'. Yet – it tickles him; it is just too nice. And moreover, he has the same archetypes in himself. So he begins to feel, 'If there are saviours, well, perhaps it is just possible that I am one', and he will fall for it, at first hesitantly, and then it will become more and more plain to him that he really is a sort of extraordinary individual. Slowly he becomes fascinated and exclusive. He is terribly touchy, susceptible, and perhaps makes himself a nuisance in medical societies. He cannot talk with his colleagues any more because he is – I don't know what. He becomes very disagreeable or withdraws from human contacts, isolates himself, and then it becomes more and more clear to him that he is a very important chap really and of great spiritual significance, probably an equal of the Mahatmas in the Himalayas, and it is quite likely that he also belongs to the great brotherhood. And then he is lost to the profession.

We have very unfortunate examples of this kind. I know quite a number of colleagues who have gone that way. They could not resist the continuous onslaught of the patients' collective unconscious – case after case projecting the saviour complex and religious expectations and the hope that perhaps this analyst with his 'secret knowledge' might own the key that has been lost by the Church, and thus could reveal the redeeming truth. All this is a subtle and very alluring temptation and they have given way to it. They identify with the archetype, they discover a creed of their own, and as they need disciples who believe in them they will found a sect.

The same problem also accounts for the peculiar difficulty psychologists of different schools have in discussing their divergent ideas in a reasonably amicable way, and for a tendency, peculiar to our branch of science, to lock themselves into little groups and scientific sects with a faith of their own. All these groups really doubt their exclusive truth, and therefore they all sit together and say the same thing continually until they finally believe it. Fanaticism is always a sign of repressed doubt. You can study that in the history of the Church. Always in those times when the Church begins to waver the style becomes fanatical, or fanatical sects spring up, because the secret doubt has to be quenched. When one is really convinced, one is perfectly calm and can discuss one's belief as a personal point of view without any particular resentment.

It is a typical occupational hazard of the psychotherapist to become psychically infected and poisoned by the projections to which he is exposed. He has to be continually on his guard against inflation. But the poison does not only affect him psychologically; it may even disturb his sympathetic system. I have observed quite a number of the most extraordinary cases of physical illness among psychotherapists, illness which does not fit in with the known medical symptomatology, and which I ascribe to the effect of this continuous onslaught of projections from which the analyst does not discriminate his own psychology. The peculiar emotional condition of the patient does have a contagious effect. One could almost say it arouses similar vibrations in the nervous system of the analyst, and therefore, like alienists, psychotherapists are apt to become a little queer. One should bear that problem in mind. It very definitely belongs to the problem of transference.

We now have to speak of the *therapy* of the transference.[4] This is an enormously difficult and complicated subject, and I am afraid I shall tell you certain things which you know just as well as I do, but in order to be systematic I cannot omit them.

It is obvious that the transference has to be dissolved and dealt with in the same way as the analyst would deal with any other projection. That means in practical terms: you have to make the patient realize the *subjective value* of the personal and impersonal contents of his transference. For it is not only personal material which he projects. As you have just heard, the contents can just as well be of an impersonal, that is archetypal, nature. The saviour complex is certainly not a personal motif; it is a world-wide expectation, an idea which you find all over the world and in every epoch of history. It is the archetypal idea of the magic personality.[5]

In the beginning of an analysis, transference projections are inevitable repetitions of former personal experiences of the patient's. At this stage you have to treat all the relationships which the patient has had before. For instance, if you have a case who has been in many health-resorts with the typical doctors you find in such places, the patient will project these experiences into the analyst; so you have first to work through the figures of all those colleagues in seaside places and sanatoria, with enormous fees and the necessary theatrical display, and the patient quite naturally assumes that you too are such a bird. You have to work through the whole series of people that the patient has experienced – the doctors, the lawyers, the teachers in schools, the uncles, the cousins, the brothers, and the father. And when you have gone through the whole procession and come right down to the nursery you think that now you are through with it, but you are not. It is just as if behind the father there was still more, and you even begin to suspect that the grandfather is being projected. That is possible; I never knew of a great-grandfather that was projected into me, but I know of a grandfather that was. When you have got down to the nursery, so that you almost peep out of the other side of existence, then you have exhausted the possibilities of *consciousness*; and if the transference does not come to an end there, despite all your efforts, it is on account of the projection of *impersonal* contents. You recognize the existence of impersonal projections by the peculiar impersonal nature of their contents; as for instance the saviour complex or an archaic God-image. The archetypal character of these images produces a 'magic', that is, an overpowering effect. With our rational consciousness we can't see why this should happen. God, for instance, is spirit, and spirit to us is nothing substantial or dynamic. But if you study the original meaning of these terms, you get at the real nature of the underlying experience, and you understand how they affect the primitive mind, and, in a similar way, the primitive psyche in ourselves. Spirit, *spiritus*, or *pneuma* really means air, wind, breath; *spiritus* and *pneuma* in their archetypal character are dynamic and half-substantial agencies; you are moved by them as by a wind, they are breathed into you, and then you are inflated.

The projected archetypal figures can just as well be of negative character, like images of the sorcerer, the devil, of demons and so on. Even analysts are not at all quite fireproof in that respect. I know colleagues who produce the most marvellous fantasies about myself and believe that I am in league with the devil and work black magic. And with people who never before thought that there was such a thing as the devil, the most incredible figures appear in the transference of impersonal contents. The projection of images of parental influence can be dissolved with the ordinary means of normal reasoning and common sense; but you cannot destroy the hold of impersonal images by mere reason. It would not even be right to destroy them, because they are tremendously important. In order to explain this, I am afraid I shall have to refer again to the history of the human mind.

It is no new discovery that archetypal images are projected. They actually have to be projected, otherwise they inundate consciousness. The problem is merely to have a form which is an adequate container. There is, as a matter of fact, an age-old institution which helps people to project impersonal images. You know it very well; you all probably have gone through the procedure, but unfortunately you were too young to recognize its importance. This institution is religious initiation, and with us it is baptism. When the fascinating and unique influence of the parental images has to be loosened, so that the child is liberated from his original biological participation with the parents, then Nature, that is the unconscious nature in man, in her infinite wisdom produces a certain kind of initiation. You find it with very primitive tribes – it is the initiation into manhood, into participation in the spiritual and social life of the tribe. In the course of the differentiation of consciousness, initiation has undergone many changes of form, until with us it was elaborated into the Christian institution of baptism. In baptism, there are two necessary functionaries, godfather and godmother. In our Swiss dialect we call them by the names of God, 'Götti' and 'Gotte'. 'Götti' is the masculine form, it means the begetter; 'Gotte' is the feminine form. The word 'God' has nothing to do with 'good'; it really means the Begetter. Baptism and the spiritual parents in the form of godfather and godmother express the mysterium of being twice-born. You know that all the higher castes in India have the honorific title of 'Twice-born'. It was also the prerogative of the Pharaoh to be twice-born. Therefore very often you find in Egyptian temples beside the main room the so-called birth-chamber where one or two rooms were reserved for the rite. In them the Pharaoh's twofold birth is described, how he is born in the flesh as a human being from ordinary parents, but is also generated by the god and carried and given birth to by the goddess. He is born the son of man and of God.

Our baptism means the detaching of the child from the merely natural parents and from the overpowering influence of the parental images. For this purpose, the biological parents are replaced by spiritual parents; godfather and godmother represent the intercessio divina through the medium of the Church, which is the visible form of the spiritual kingdom. In the Catholic rite even marriage – where we should suppose it to be all-important that this particular man and this particular woman become united and are confronted with each other – is interfered with by the Church; the intercessio sacerdotis prevents the immediate contact of the couple. The priest represents the Church, and the Church is always in between in the form of confession, which is obligatory. This intervention is not due to the particular cunning of the Church; it is rather her great wisdom, and it is an idea going back to the very origins of Christianity that we are not married merely as man and woman; we are married in Christo. I own an antique vase upon which an early Christian marriage is represented. The man and the woman hold each other's hand in the Fish; the Fish is between them, and the Fish is Christ. In this way the couple is united in the Fish. They are separated and united by Christ; Christ is in between, he is the representative of the power which is meant to separate man from merely natural forces.

This process of separation from nature is undergone in the well-known initiation rites or puberty rites of primitive tribes. When they approach puberty, the boys are called away suddenly. In the night they hear the voice of the spirits, the bull-roarers, and no woman is allowed to appear out of the house, or she is killed instantly. Then the boys are brought out to the bush-house, where they are put through all sorts of gruesome performances. They are not allowed to speak; they are told that they are dead, and then they are told that they are now reborn. They are given new names in order to prove that they are no more the same personalities as before, and so they are no longer the children of their parents. The initiation can even go so far that, after they return, the mothers are not allowed to talk to their sons any more, because the young men are no longer their children. Formerly, with the Hottentots, the boy had occasionally even to perform incest once with his mother in order to prove that she was not his mother any more, but just a woman like the rest.

Our corresponding Christian rite has lost much of its importance; but if you study the symbolism of baptism you still see traces of the original meaning. Our birth-chamber is the baptismal font; this is really the piscina, the fish-pond in which one is like a little fish: one is symbolically drowned and then revived. You know that the early Christians were actually plunged into the baptismal font, and this used to be much larger than it is now; in many old churches the baptistry was a building on its own, and it was always built on the ground-plan of a circle. On the day before Easter, the Catholic Church has a special ceremony for the consecration of the baptismal font, the Benedictio Fontis. The merely natural water is exorcised from the admixture of all malign powers and transformed into the regenerating and purifying fountain of life, the immaculate womb of the divine source. Then the priest divides the water in the fourfold form of the cross, breathes upon it three times, plunges the consecrated Easter candle three times into it, as a symbol of the eternal light, and at the same time his incantation brings the virtue, the power of the Spiritus Sanctus to descend into the font. From this hierosgamos, from the holy marriage between the Spiritus Sanctus and the baptismal water as the womb of the Church, man is reborn in the true innocence of new childhood. The maculation of sin is taken from him and his nature is joined with the image of God. He is no longer contaminated by merely natural forces, he is regenerated as a spiritual being.

We know of other institutions for detaching man from natural conditions. I can't go into much detail, but if you study the psychology of primitives, you find that all important events of life are connected with elaborate ceremonies whose purpose is to detach man from the preceding stage of existence and to help him to transfer his psychic energy into the next phase. When a girl marries, she ought to be detached from the parental images and should not become attached to a projection of the father-image into the husband. Therefore in Babylon a peculiar ritual was observed whose purpose was to detach the young girl from the father-image. This is the rite of temple prostitution, in which girls of good families had to hand themselves over to a stranger visiting the temple, who presumably would never return, and had to spend a night with him. We know of a similar institution in the Middle Ages, the jus primae noctis, the right of the first night which the feudal lord had in regard to his serfs. The bride had to spend her wedding-night with her feudal lord. By the rite of temple prostitution, a most impressive image was created which collided with the image of the man the young woman was going to marry, and so when there was trouble in marriage – for even in those days trouble occasionally arose – the regression which is the natural result would not go back to the father-image but to the stranger she had once met, the lover who came from unknown lands. Then she did not fall back into childhood but upon a human being suited to her age, and so was sufficiently protected against infantile regression.

This ritual shows a very beautiful observation of the human psyche. For there is an archetypal image in women of a lover in a remote, unknown land, a man coming over the seas who meets her once and then goes away again. You know this motif from Wagner's Flying Dutchman and from Ibsen's Lady from the Sea. In both dramas the heroine is waiting for the stranger who will come from far over the seas to have the great love experience with her. In Wagner's opera she has fallen in love with the actual image of him and knows him even before he arrives. The Lady from the Sea has met him once before and is under the compulsion of always going to the sea to await his return. In that Babylonian rite this archetypal image is lived concretely in order to detach the woman from the parental images which are real archetypal images and therefore exceedingly powerful. I have written a little book about the relations between the ego and the unconscious,[6] where I have described a case of projection of the father-image by a woman who was under my treatment, and how the problem then developed through the analysis of the archetypal image which was at the basis of this father transference.

The first stage of the treatment of the transference does not involve only the realization by the patient that he is still looking at the world from the angle of the nursery, school-room, and so on, by projecting and expecting all the positive and negative authoritative figures of his personal experience; this realization merely deals with the objective side. To establish a really mature attitude, he has to see the subjective value of all these images which seem to create trouble for him. He has to assimilate them into his own psychology; he has to find out in what way they are part of himself; how he attributes for instance a positive value to an object, when as a matter of fact it is he who could and should develop this value. And in the same way, when he projects negative qualities and therefore hates and loathes the object, he has to discover that he is projecting his own inferior side, his shadow, as it were, because he prefers to have an optimistic and one-sided image of himself. Freud, as you know, deals only with the objective side. But you cannot really help a patient to assimilate the contents of his neurosis by indulgence in a childish lack of responsibility, or by resignation to a blind fate of which he is the victim. His neurosis means him to become a total personality, and that includes recognition of and responsibility for his whole being, his good and his bad sides, his superior as well as his inferior functions.

Let us now assume that the projection of personal images has been worked through and is sufficiently dealt with, but there is still a transference which you simply cannot dissolve. Then we come to the *second stage* in the therapy of transference. That is the *discrimination between personal and impersonal contents*. The personal projections, as we have seen, must be dissolved; and they can be dissolved through conscious realization. But the impersonal projections cannot be destroyed because they belong to the structural elements of the psyche. They are not relics of a past which has to be outgrown; they are, on the contrary, purposive and compensatory functions of the utmost importance. They are an important protection against situations in which a man might lose his head. In any situation of panic, whether external or internal, the archetypes intervene and allow a man to react in an instinctively adapted way, just as if he had always known the situation: he reacts in the way mankind has always reacted. Therefore the mechanism is of vital importance.

It goes without saying that the projection of these impersonal images upon the analyst has to be withdrawn. But you merely dissolve the *act* of projection; you should not, and really cannot, dissolve its *contents*. Neither, of course, can the patient assimilate the impersonal contents into his personal psychology. The fact that they are *impersonal* contents is just the reason for projecting them; one feels that they do not belong to one's subjective mind, they must be located somewhere outside one's ego, and, for lack of a suitable form, a human object is made their receptacle. So you have to be exceedingly careful in handling impersonal projections. It would, for instance, be a great mistake to say to a patient: 'You see, you simply project the saviour-image into me. What nonsense to expect a saviour and to make me responsible'. If you meet such an expectation, take it seriously; it is by no means nonsense. The whole world has a saviour expectation; you find it everywhere. Look at Italy, for instance, or look at Germany. At present you have no saviour in England, and in Switzerland we have none; but I don't believe that we are so very different from the rest of Europe. The situation with us is slightly different from that of the Italians and Germans; they are perhaps a little bit less balanced; but even with us it would need precious little. In those countries you have the saviour complex as mass psychology. The saviour complex is an archetypal image of the collective unconscious, and it quite naturally becomes activated in an epoch so full of trouble and disorientation as ours. In these collective events, we merely see, as through a magnifying glass, what can also happen within the individual. It is in just such a moment of panic that the compensatory psychic elements come into action. It is not at all an abnormal phenomenon. It is perhaps strange to us that it should be expressed in political form. But the collective unconscious is a very irrational factor, and our rational consciousness cannot dictate to it how it should make its appearance. Of course, if left entirely to itself, its activation can be very destructive; it can, for instance, be a psychosis. Therefore, man's relation to the collective unconscious has always been regulated; there is a characteristic form by which the archetypal images are expressed. For the collective unconscious is a function that always operates, and man has to keep in touch with it. His psychic and spiritual health is dependent on the co-operation of the impersonal images. Therefore man has always had his religions.

What are religions? Religions are psychotherapeutic systems. What are we doing, we psychotherapists? We are trying to heal the suffering of the human mind, of the human psyche or the human soul, and religions deal with the same problem. Therefore our Lord himself is a healer; he is a doctor; he heals the sick and he deals with the troubles of the soul; and that is exactly what we call psychotherapy. It is not a play on words when I call religion a psycho-therapeutic system. It is the most elaborate system, and there is a great prac-tical truth behind it. I have a clientele which is pretty large and extends over a number of continents, and where I live we are practically surrounded by Catholics; but during the last thirty years I have not had more than about six practising Catholics among my patients. The vast majority were Protestants and Jews. I once sent round a questionnaire to people whom I did not know, asking: 'If you were in psychological trouble what would you do? Would you go to the doctor or would you go to the priest or parson?' I cannot remember the actual figures; but I remember that about twenty per cent of the Protestants said they would go to the parson. All the rest were most emphatically against the parson and for the doctor, and the most emphatic were the relatives and children of parsons. There was one Chinese who replied, and he put it very nicely. He remarked: 'When I am young I go to the doctor, and when I am old I go to the philosopher'. But about fifty-eight or sixty per cent of the Catholics answered that they would certainly go to the priest. That proves that the Catholic Church in particular, with its rigorous system of confession and its director of conscience, is a therapeutic institution. I have had some patients who, after having had analysis with me, even joined the Catholic Church, just as I have had some patients who now go to the so-called Oxford Group Movement – with my blessing! I think it is perfectly correct to make use of these psychotherapeutic institutions which history has given to us, and I wish I were still a medieval man who could join such a creed. Unfortunately it needs a somewhat medieval psychology to do it, and I am not sufficiently medieval. But you see from this that I take the archetypal images and a suitable form for their projection seriously, because the collective unconscious is really a serious factor in the human psyche.

All those personal things like incestuous tendencies and other childish tunes are mere surface; what the unconscious really contains are the great collective events of the time. In the collective unconscious of the individual, history prepares itself; and when the archetypes are activated in a number of individuals and come to the surface, we are in the midst of history, as we are at present. The archetypal image which the moment requires gets into life, and everybody is seized by it. That is what we see today. I saw it coming, I said in 1918 that the 'blond beast' is stirring in its sleep and that something will happen in Germany.[7] No psychologist then understood at all what I meant, because people had simply no idea that our personal psychology is just a thin skin, a ripple upon the ocean of collective psychology. The powerful factor, the factor which changes our whole life, which changes the surface of our known world, which makes history, is collective psychology, and collective psychology moves according to laws entirely different from those of our consciousness. The archetypes are the great decisive forces, they bring about the real events, and not our personal reasoning and practical intellect. Before the Great War all intelligent people said: 'We shall not have any more war, we are far too reasonable to let it happen, and our commerce and finance are so interlaced internationally that war is absolutely out of the question'. And then we produced the most gorgeous war ever seen. And now they begin to talk that foolish kind of talk about reason and peace plans and such things; they blindfold themselves by clinging to a childish optimism – and now look at reality! Sure enough, the archetypal images decide the fate of man. Man's unconscious psychology decides, and not what we think and talk in the brain-chamber up in the attic.

Who would have thought in 1900 that it would be possible thirty years later for such things to happen in Germany as are happening today? Would you have believed that a whole nation of highly intelligent and cultivated people could be seized by the fascinating power of an archetype? I saw it coming, and I can understand it because I know the power of the collective unconscious. But on the surface it looks simply incredible. Even my personal friends are under that fascination, and when I am in Germany, I believe it myself, I understand it all, I know it has to be as it is. One cannot resist it. It gets you below the belt and not in your mind, your brain just counts for nothing, your sympathetic system is gripped. It is a power that fascinates people from within, it is the collective unconscious which is activated, it is an archetype which is common to them all that has come to life. And because it is an archetype, it has historical aspects and we cannot understand the events without knowing history.[8] It is German history that is being lived today, just as Fascism is living Italian history. We cannot be children about it, having intellectual and reasonable ideas and saying: this should not be. That is just childish. This is real history, this is what really happens to man and has always happened, and it is far more important than our personal little woes and our personal convictions. I know highly educated Germans who were just as reasonable as I think I am or as you think you are. But a wave went over them and just washed their reason away, and when you talk to them you have to admit that they could not do anything about it. An incomprehensible fate has seized them, and you cannot say it is right, or it is wrong. It has nothing to do with rational judgment, it is just history. And when your patient's transference touches upon the archetypes, you touch upon a mine that may explode, just as we see it explode collectively. These impersonal images contain enormous dynamic power. Bernard Shaw says in *Man and Superman*: 'This creature Man, who in his own selfish affairs is a coward to the backbone, will fight for an idea like a hero'.[9] Of course, we would not call Fascism or Hitlerism ideas. They are archetypes, and so we would say: Give an archetype to the people and the whole crowd moves like one man, there is no resisting it.

On account of this tremendous dynamic power of archetypal images you cannot reason them away. Therefore the only thing to do at the *third stage* of the therapy of the transference is *to differentiate the personal relationship to the analyst from impersonal factors*. It is perfectly understandable that when you have carefully and honestly worked for a patient, he likes you, and because you have done a decent bit of work on a patient, you like him, whether it is a man or a woman. That is quite self-evident. It would be most unnatural and neurotic if there were not some personal recognition on the patient's part for what you have done for him. A personal human reaction to you is normal and reasonable, therefore let it be, it deserves to live; it is not transference any more. But such an attitude to the analyst is possible in a human and decent form only when it is not vitiated by unrecognized impersonal values. This means that there has to be, on the other side, a full recognition of the importance of the archetypal images, many of which have a religious character. Whether you assume that the Nazi storm in Germany has a religious value or not does not matter. It has. Whether you think that the Duce is a religious figure or not does not matter, because he is a religious figure. You could even read the affirmation of it in a newspaper these days, when they quoted that verse about a Roman Caesar: 'Ecce deus, deus ille, Menalca'.[10] Fascism is the Latin form of religion, and its religious character explains why the whole thing has such a tremendous fascination.

The consequence of this recognition of the importance of impersonal values may be that your patient joins a Church or a religious creed or whatever it may be. If he cannot bring together his experience of the collective unconscious within a given religious form, then the difficulty begins. Then the impersonal factors have no receptacle, and so the patient falls back into the transference, and the archetypal images spoil the human relation to the analyst. Then the analyst is the saviour, or curse him, he is not when he ought to be! For he is only a human being; he cannot be the saviour nor any other archetypal image which is activated in the patient's unconscious.

On account of that enormously difficult and important problem I have worked out a particular technique for restoring these projected impersonal values to the individual himself. It is a rather complicated technique, and last night I was just about to show you something of it in relation to that dream. For when the unconscious says that below the Christian Church is the secret chamber with the golden bowl and the golden dagger, it does not lie. The unconscious is nature, and nature never lies. There is gold, there is the treasure and the great value.

If I had had the opportunity I would have gone on and told you something about that treasure and the means to secure it. And then you would have seen the justification for the method which enables the individual to keep in touch with his impersonal images. As it is, I can only allude to it and must refer you to my books for further material.[11]

I call this fourth stage of the therapy of transference the *objectivation of impersonal images*. It is an essential part of the process of individuation.[12] Its goal is to detach consciousness from the object so that the individual no longer places the guarantee of his happiness, or of his life even, in factors outside himself, whether they be persons, ideas, or circumstances, but comes to realize that everything depends on whether he holds the treasure or not. If the possession of that gold is realized, then the centre of gravity is in the individual and no longer in an object on which he depends. To reach such a condition of detachment is the aim of Eastern practices, and it is also the aim of all the teachings of the Church. In the various religions the treasure is projected into the sacred figures, but this hypostasis is no longer possible for the modern enlightened mind. A great number of individuals cannot express their impersonal values in historical symbols any more.

They are therefore faced with the necessity of finding an individual method by which the impersonal images are given shape. For they have to take on form, they have to live their characteristic life, otherwise the individual is severed from the basic function of the psyche, and then he is neurotic, he is disorientated and in conflict with himself. But if he is able to objectify the impersonal images and relate to them, he is in touch with that vital psychological function which from the dawn of consciousness has been taken care of by religion.

It is impossible for me to go into details of the problem, not only because the time for my lecture is over, but because it is beyond scientific conceptions to give adequate expression to a living psychic experience. All we can say rationally about this condition of detachment is to define it as a sort of centre within the psyche of the individual, but not within the ego. It is a non-ego centre. I am afraid I should have to give you a long dissertation on comparative religion in order to convey to you fully what I mean by a non-ego centre.[13] So I can only mention the existence of this problem. It is really the essential problem of a great number of individuals who come to analysis, and therefore the psychotherapist has to try to find a method by which he can help them to solve it.

If we adopt such a method, we take up the torch that was abandoned by our old colleagues of the seventeenth century when they put it down in order to become chemists. In so far as we psychologists are emerging from chemical and material conceptions of the psyche, we are taking up that torch again, continuing a process which began in the West in the twelfth century – for alchemy was the work of the doctors who were busy with the mind.

DISCUSSION

Question:

May I ask Professor Jung a very elementary question: Would he give us a definition of neurosis?

Professor Jung:

A neurosis is a dissociation of personality due to the existence of complexes. To have complexes is in itself normal; but if the complexes are incompatible, that part of the personality which is too contrary to the conscious part becomes split off. If the split reaches the organic structure, the dissociation is a psychosis, a schizophrenic condition, as the term denotes. Each complex then lives an existence of its own, with no personality left to tie them together.

As the split-off complexes are unconscious, they find only an indirect means of expression, that is, through neurotic symptoms. Instead of suffering from a psychological conflict, one suffers from a neurosis. Any incompatibility of character can cause dissociation, and too great a split between the thinking and the feeling function, for instance, is already a slight neurosis. When you are not quite at one with yourself in a given matter, you are approaching a neurotic condition. The idea of psychic dissociation is the most general and cautious way I can define a neurosis. Of course it does not cover the symptomatology and phenomenology of neurosis; it is only the most general psychological formulation I am able to give.

Dr H. G. Baynes:

You said that transference is of no practical value in analysis. Is it not possible to give it a teleological value?

Professor Jung:

I have not said it in so many words, but the teleological value of transference becomes apparent from an analysis of its archetypal contents. Its purposive value is also shown in what I said about transference as a function of compensation for a lack of rapport between the analyst and the patient – at least if one assumes that it is normal for human beings to be *en rapport* with each other. Of course I could imagine that an introverted philosopher is rather inclined to think that people have no contacts. For instance, Schopenhauer says that human egotism is so great that a man can kill his brother in order to smear his boots with his brother's fat.

Dr Henry V. Dicks:

I think we can assume then, Professor Jung, that you regard the outbreak of a neurosis as an attempt at self-cure, as an attempt at compensation by bringing out the inferior function?

Professor Jung:

Absolutely.

Dr Dicks:

I understand, then, that the outbreak of a neurotic illness, from the point of view of man's development, is something favourable?

Professor Jung:

That is so, and I am glad you bring up that idea. That is really my point of view. I am not altogether pessimistic about neurosis. In many cases we have to say: 'Thank heaven he could make up his mind to be neurotic'. Neurosis is really an attempt at self-cure, just as any physical disease is partly an attempt at self-cure. We cannot understand a disease as an *ens per se* any more, as something detached which not so long ago it was believed to be. Modern medicine – internal medicine, for instance – conceives of disease as a system composed of a harmful factor and a healing factor. It is exactly the same with neurosis. It is an attempt of the self-regulating psychic system to restore the balance, in no way different from the function of dreams – only rather more forceful and drastic.

Dr J. A. Hadfield:

Would Professor Jung give us a short account of the technique of active imagination?

Professor Jung:

That was the subject I really wanted to tell you about today in consequence of the analysis of the Toledo dream, so I am very glad to take it up. You will realize that I shall not be able to present any empirical material, but I may succeed in giving you an idea of the method. I believe that the best way is to tell you of a case where it was very difficult to teach the patient the method.

I was treating a young artist, and he had the greatest trouble in understanding what I meant by active imagination. He tried all sorts of things but he could not get at it. The difficulty with him was that he could not think. Musicians, painters, artists of all kinds, often can't think at all, because they never intentionally use their brain. This man's brain too was always working for itself; it had its artistic imaginations and he couldn't use it psychologically, so he couldn't understand. I gave him every chance to try, and he tried all sorts of stunts. I cannot tell you all the things he did, but I will tell you how he finally succeeded in using his imagination psychologically.

I live outside the town, and he had to take the train to get to my place. It starts from a small station, and on the wall of that station was a poster. Each time he waited for his train he looked at that poster. The poster was an advertisement for Mürren in the Bernese Alps, a colourful picture of the waterfalls, of a green meadow and a hill in the centre, and on that hill were several cows. So he sat there staring at that poster and thinking that he could not find out what I meant by active imagination. And then one day he thought: 'Perhaps I could start by having a fantasy about that poster. I might for instance imagine that I am myself in the poster, that the scenery is real and that I could walk up the hill among the cows and then look down on the other side, and then I might see what there is behind that hill'.

So he went to the station for that purpose and imagined that he was in the poster. He saw the meadow and the road and walked up the hill among the cows, and then he came up to the top and looked down, and there was the meadow again, sloping down, and below was a hedge with a stile. So he walked down and over the stile, and there was a little footpath that ran round a ravine, and a rock, and when he came round that rock, there was a small chapel, with its door standing a little ajar. He thought he would like to enter, and so he pushed the door open and went in, and there upon an altar decorated with pretty flowers stood a wooden figure of the Mother of God. He looked up at her face, and in that exact moment something with pointed ears disappeared behind the altar. He thought, 'Well, that's all nonsense', and instantly the whole fantasy was gone.

He went away and said, 'Now again I haven't understood what active imagination is'. And then, suddenly, the thought struck him: 'Well, perhaps that really *was* there; perhaps that thing behind the Mother of God, with the pointed ears, that disappeared like a flash, really happened'. Therefore he said to himself: 'I will just try it all over as a test'. So he imagined that he was back in the station looking at the poster, and again he fantasised that he was walking up the hill. And when he came to the top of the hill, he wondered what he would see on the other side. And there was the hedge and the stile and the hill sloping down. He said, 'Well, so far so good. Things haven't moved since, apparently'. And he went round the rock, and there was the chapel. He said: 'There is the chapel, that at least is no illusion. It is all quite in order'. The door stood ajar and he was quite pleased. He hesitated a moment and said: 'Now, when I push that door open and I see the Madonna on the altar, then that thing with the pointed ears should jump down behind the Madonna, and if it doesn't, then the whole thing is bunk!' And so he pushed the door open and looked – and there it all was and the thing jumped down, as before, and then he was convinced. From then on he had the key and knew he could rely on his imagination, and so he learned to use it.

There is no time to tell you about the development of his images, nor how other patients arrive at the method. For of course everybody gets at it in his own way. I can only mention that it might also be a dream or an impression of a hypnagogic nature from which active imagination can start. I really prefer the term 'imagination' to 'fantasy', because there is a difference between the two which the old doctors had in mind when they said that 'opus nostrum', our work, ought to be done 'per veram imaginationem et non phantastica' – by true imagination and not by a fantastical one.[14] In other words, if you take the correct meaning of this definition, fantasy is mere nonsense, a phantasm, a fleeting impression; but imagination is active, purposeful creation. And this is exactly the distinction I make too.

A fantasy is more or less your own invention, and remains on the surface of personal things and conscious expectations. But active imagination, as the term denotes, means that the images have a life of their own and that the symbolic events develop according to their own logic – that is, of course, if your conscious reason does not interfere. You begin by concentrating upon a starting point. I will give you an example from my own experience. When I was a little boy, I had a spinster aunt who lived in a nice old-fashioned house. It was full of beautiful old coloured engravings. Among them was a picture of my grandfather on my mother's side. He was a sort of bishop, and he was represented as coming out of his house and standing on a little terrace. There were handrails and stairs coming down from the terrace, and a footpath leading to the cathedral. He was in full regalia, standing there at the top of the terrace. Every Sunday morning I was allowed to pay a call on my aunt, and then I knelt on a chair and looked at that picture until grandfather came down the steps. And each time my aunt would say, 'But, my dear, he doesn't walk, he is still standing there'. But I knew I had seen him walking down.

You see how it happened that the picture began to move. And in the same way, when you concentrate on a mental picture, it begins to stir, the image becomes enriched by details, it moves and develops. Each time, naturally, you mistrust it and have the idea that you have just made it up, that it is merely your own invention. But you have to overcome that doubt, because it is not true. We can really produce precious little by our conscious mind. All the time we are dependent upon the things that literally fall into our consciousness; therefore in German we call them Einfälle. For instance, if my unconscious should prefer not to give me ideas, I could not proceed with my lecture, because I could not invent the next step. You all know the experience when you want to mention a name or a word which you know quite well, and it simply does not present itself; but some time later it drops into your memory. We depend entirely upon the benevolent co-operation of our unconscious. If it does not co-operate, we are completely lost. Therefore I am convinced that we cannot do much in the way of conscious invention; we over-estimate the power of intention and the will. And so when we concentrate on an inner picture and when we are careful not to interrupt the natural flow of events, our unconscious will produce a series of images which make a complete story.

I have tried that method with many patients and for many years, and I possess a large collection of such 'opera'. It is most interesting to watch the process. Of course I don't use active imagination as a panacea; there have to be definite indications that the method is suitable for the individual, and there are a number of patients with whom it would be wrong to force it upon them. But often in the later stages of analysis, the objectivation of images replaces the dreams. The images anticipate the dreams, and so the dream-material begins to peter out. The unconscious becomes deflated in so far as the conscious mind relates to it. Then you get all the material in a creative form and this has great advantages over dream-material. It quickens the process of maturation, for analysis is a process of quickened maturation. This definition is not my own invention; the old professor Stanley Hall invented the term.

Since by active imagination all the material is produced in a conscious state of mind, the material is far more rounded out than the dreams with their precarious language. And it contains much more than dreams do; for instance, the feeling-values are in it, and one can judge it by feeling. Quite often, the patients themselves feel that certain material contains a tendency to visibility. They say, for instance: 'That dream was so impressive, if I only could paint I would try to express its atmosphere'. Or they feel that a certain idea should be expressed not rationally but in symbols. Or they are gripped by an emotion which, if given form, would be explainable, and so on. And so they begin to draw, to paint, or to shape their images plastically, and women sometimes do weaving. I have even had one or two women who danced their unconscious figures. Of course, they can also be expressed in writing.

I have many long series of such pictures. They yield an enormous amount of archetypal material. Just now I am about to work out the historical parallels of some of them. I compare them with the pictorial material produced in similar attempts in past centuries, particularly in the early Middle Ages. Certain elements of the symbolism go back to Egypt. In the East we find many interesting parallels to our unconscious material, even down to the last details. This comparative work gives us a most valuable insight into the structure of the unconscious. You have to hand the necessary parallels to the patients too, not of course in such an elaborate way as you would present it in a scientific study, but as much as each individual needs in order to understand his archetypal images. For he can see their real meaning only when they are not just a queer subjective experience with no external connections, but a typical, ever-recurring expression of the objective facts and processes of the human psyche. By objectifying his impersonal images, and understanding their inherent ideas, the patient is able to work out all the values of his archetypal material. Then he can really see it, and the unconscious becomes understandable to him. Moreover, this work has a definite effect upon him. Whatever he has put into it works back on him and produces a change of attitude which I tried to define by mentioning the non-ego centre.

I will give you an interesting example. I had a case, a university man, a very one-sided intellectual. His unconscious had become troubled and activated; so it projected itself into other men who appeared to be his enemies, and he felt terribly lonely, because everybody seemed to be against him. Then he began to drink in order to forget his troubles, but he got exceedingly irritable and in these moods he began to quarrel with other men, and several times he had very disagreeable encounters, and once he was thrown out of a restaurant and got beaten up. And there were more incidents of that sort. Then things became really too thick for his endurance, and he came to me to ask my advice about what he should do. In that interview, I got a very definite impression of him: I saw that he was chock-full of archaic material, and I said to myself: 'Now I am going to make an interesting experiment to get that material absolutely pure, without any influence from myself, and therefore I won't touch it'. So I sent him to a woman doctor who was then just a beginner and who did not know much about archetypal material. Thus I was absolutely sure that she would not tamper with it. The patient was in such low spirits that he did not object to my proposition. So he worked with her and did everything she said.[15]

She told him to watch his dreams, and he wrote them all down carefully, from the first to the last. I now have a series of about thirteen hundred dreams of his. They contain the most marvellous series of archetypal images. And quite naturally, without being told to do so, he began to draw a number of pictures which he saw in his dreams, because he felt them to be very important. And in this work on his dreams and on these pictures he did exactly the kind of work which other patients do by active imagination. He even invented active imagination for himself in order to work out certain most intricate problems which his dreams presented him with, as for instance how to balance the contents of a circle, and more things like this. He worked out the problem of the *perpetuum mobile*, not in a crazy way but in a symbolic way. He worked on all the problems which medieval philosophy was so keen on and of which our rational mind says, 'That is all nonsense'. Such a statement only shows that we do not understand. They did understand; we are the fools, not they.

In the course of this analysis, which took him through about the first four hundred dreams, he was not under my surveillance. After the first interview I did not see him at all for eight months. He was five months with that doctor, and then for three months he was doing the work all by himself, continuing the observation of his unconscious with minute accuracy. He was very gifted in this respect. In the end, for about two months, he had a number of interviews with me. But I did not have to explain much of the symbolism to him.

The effect of this work with his unconscious was that he became a perfectly normal and reasonable person. He did not drink any more, he became completely adapted and in every respect completely normal. The reason for this is quite obvious: that man – he was not married – had lived in a very one-sided intellectual way, and naturally had certain desires and needs also. But he had no chance with women at all, because he had no differentiation of feeling whatsoever. So he made a fool of himself with women at once, and of course they had no patience with him. And he made himself very disagreeable to men, so he was frightfully lonely. But now he had found something that fascinated him; he had a new centre of interest. He soon discovered that his dreams pointed to something very meaningful, and so his whole intuitive and scientific interest was aroused. Instead of feeling like a lost sheep, he thought: 'Ah, when I am through with my work in the evening, I go to my study, and then I shall see what happens. I will work over my dreams, and then I shall discover extraordinary things'. And so it was. Of course rational judgment would say that he just fell violently into his fantasies. But that was not the case at all. He did a real bit of hard work on his unconscious, and he worked out his images scientifically. When he came to me after his three months alone, he was already almost normal. Only he still felt uncertain; he was troubled because he could not understand some of the material he had dug up from the unconscious. He asked my advice about it, and I most carefully gave him certain hints as to its meaning, but only so far as this could help him to keep on with the work and carry it through.

At the end of the year I am going to publish a selection from his first four hundred dreams, where I show the development of one motif only, the central motif of these archetypal images.[16] There will be an English translation later, and then you will have the opportunity to see how the method works in a case absolutely untouched by myself, or by any other outside suggestion. It is a most amazing series of images and really shows what active imagination can do. You understand, in this case it was only partially a method for objectifying the images in plastic form, because many of the symbols appeared directly in the dreams; but all the same it shows the kind of atmosphere which active imagination can produce. I have patients who, evening after evening, work at these images, painting and shaping their observations and experiences. The work has a fascination for them; it is the fascination which the archetypes always exert upon consciousness. But by objectifying them, the danger of their inundating consciousness is averted and their positive effect is made accessible. It is almost impossible to define this effect in rational terms; it is a sort of 'magical' effect, that is, a suggestive influence which goes out from the images to the individual, and in this way his unconscious is extended and is changed.

I am told that Dr Bennet has brought some pictures by a patient. Will he be so kind as to show them?

The picture (Figure 14) is meant to represent a bowl or vase. Of course it is very clumsily expressed and is a mere attempt, a suggestion of a vase or bowl. The motif of the vessel is itself an archetypal image which has a certain purpose, and I can prove from this picture what the purpose is. A vessel is an instrument for containing things. It contains for instance liquids, and prevents them from getting dispersed. Our German word for vessel is *Gefäss*, which is the noun of *fassen*, that is, to set, to contain, to take hold of. The word *Fassung* means the setting, and also, metaphorically, composure, to remain collected. So the vessel in this picture indicates the movement of containing in order to gather in and to hold together. You have to hold something together which otherwise would fall asunder. From the way this picture is composed, and from certain features in it, it is obvious that the psychology of this man contains a number of disparate elements. It is a picture characteristic of a schizophrenic condition. I do not know the case at all, but Dr Bennet confirms that my conclusion is correct. You see the disparate elements all over the picture; there are a number of things which are not

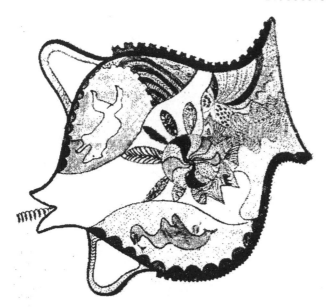

Figure 14 Painting by a patient

motivated and which don't belong together. Moreover, you see peculiar lines dividing the field. These lines are characteristic of a schizophrenic mentality; I call them the breaking lines. When a schizophrenic paints a picture of himself, he naturally expresses the schizophrenic split in his own mental structure, and so you find these breaking lines which often go right through a particular figure, like the breaking lines in a mirror. In this picture, the figures themselves show no breaking lines; they only go all over the field.

This man, then, tries to gather in all the disparate elements into the vessel. The vessel is meant to be the receptacle for his whole being, for all the incompatible units. If he tried to gather them into his ego, it would be an impossible task, because the ego can be identical only with one part at a time. So he indicates by the symbol of the vessel that he is trying to find a container for everything, and therefore he gives a hint at a non-ego centre by that sort of ball or globe in the middle.

The picture is an attempt at self-cure. It brings all the disparate elements into the light, and it also tries to put them together into that vessel. This idea of a receptacle is an archetypal idea. You find it everywhere, and it is one of the central motifs of unconscious pictures. It is the idea of the magic circle which is drawn round something that has to be prevented from escaping or protected against hostile influences. The magic circle as an apotropaic charm is an archaic idea which you still find in folklore. For instance, if a man digs for a treasure, he draws the magic circle round the field in order to keep the devil out. When the ground-plan of a city was set out, there used to be a ritual walk or ride round the circumference in order to protect the place within. In some Swiss villages, it is still the custom for the priest and the town council to ride round the fields when the blessing is administered for the protection of the harvest. In the centre of the magic circle or sacred precinct is the temple. One of the most wonderful examples of this idea is the temple of Borobudur in Java. The walk round, the *circumambulatio*, is done in a spiral; the pilgrims pass the figures of all the different lives of the Buddha, until on the top there is the invisible Buddha, the Buddha yet to come. The ground-plan of Borobudur is a circle within a square. This structure is called in Sanskrit a mandala. The word means a circle, particularly a magic circle. In the East, you find the mandala not only as the ground-plan of temples, but as pictures in the temples, or drawn for the day of certain religious festivals. In the very centre of the mandala there is the god, or the symbol of divine energy, the diamond thunderbolt. Round this innermost circle is a cloister with four gates. Then comes a garden, and round this there is another circle which is the outer circumference.

The symbol of the mandala has exactly this meaning of a holy place, a *temenos*, to protect the centre. And it is a symbol which is one of the most important motifs in the objectivation of unconscious images.[17] It is a means of protecting the centre of the personality from being drawn out and from being influenced from outside.

This picture by Dr Bennet's patient is an attempt to draw such a mandala. It has a centre, and it contains all his psychic elements, and the vase would be the magic circle, the *temenos*, round which he has to do the *circumambulatio*. Attention is thus directed towards the centre, and at the same time all the disparate elements come under observation and an attempt is made to unify them. The *circumambulatio* had always to be done clockwise. If one turned round in the other direction it was very unfavourable. The idea of the *circumambulatio* in this picture is the patient's first attempt to find a centre and a container for his whole psyche. But he does not succeed. The design shows no balance, and the vase is toppling over. It even topples over towards the left, towards the side of the unconscious. So the unconscious is still too powerful. If he wants his apotropaic magic to work, he must do it in a different way. We shall see what he does in the next picture.

In this picture (Figure 15) he makes an attempt at symmetry. Now these disparate, monstrous things which he could not grasp before are collected and assimilated into more favourable, less pathological forms. He can now gather the living units of his unconscious, in the form of snakes, into the

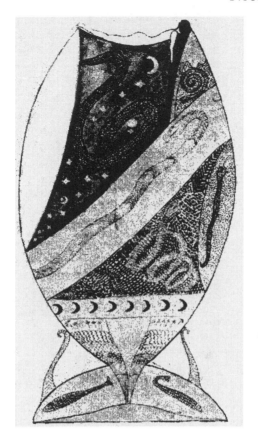

Figure 15 Painting by a patient

sacred vase. And the vase stands firm, it does not topple over any more, and its shape has improved. He does not succeed yet with his intention; but at least he can give his animals some form. They are all animals of the under-world, fishes that live in the deep sea, and snakes of the darkness. They symbolize the lower centres of his psychology, the sympathetic system. A most remarkable thing is that he also gathers in the stars. That means that the cosmos, his world, is collected into the picture. It is an allusion to the uncon-scious astrology which is in our bones, though we are unaware of it. At the top of the whole picture is the personification of the unconscious, a naked anima-figure who turns her back. That is a typical position; in the beginning of the objectivation of these images the anima-figure often turns her back. At the foot of the vase are eight figures of the crescent moon; the moon is also a symbol of the unconscious. A man's unconscious is the lunar world, for it is the night world, and this is characterized by the moon, and Luna is a feminine designation, because the unconscious is feminine. There are still various breaking lines which disturb the harmony. But I should assume that if no particular trouble interferes, the patient will most likely continue along this constructive line. I should say that there is hope that he might come round altogether, because the appearance of the anima is rather a positive sign. She also is a sort of vase, for in the beginning she incorporates the whole of the unconscious, instead of its being scattered in all the various units. Also, the patient tries to separate the motifs to the right and to the left, and this indicates an attempt at conscious orientation. The ball or globe in the first picture has disappeared, but this is not a negative sign. The whole vessel is the centre, and he has corrected the toppling over of the vase, it stands quite firmly on its base. All this shows that he is really making an attempt to put himself right.

The pictures should be given back to the patient because they are very important. You can get copies; patients like to do copies for the doctor. But he should leave the originals with the patients, because they want to look at them; and when they look at them they feel that their unconscious is expressed. The objective form works back on them and they become enchanted. The suggestive influence of the picture reacts on the psychological system of the patient and induces the same effect which he put into the picture. That is the reason for idols, for the magic use of sacred images, of icons. They cast their magic into our system and put us right, provided we put ourselves into them. If you put yourself into the icon, the icon will speak to you. Take a Lamaic mandala which has a Buddha in the centre, or a Shiva, and, to the extent that you can put yourself into it, it answers and comes into you. It has a magic effect.

Because these pictures of the unconscious express the actual psychological condition of the individual, you can use them for the purpose of diagnosis. You can tell right away from such a picture where the patient stands, whether he has a schizophrenic disposition or is merely neurotic. You can even tell what his prognosis is. It only needs some experience to make these paintings exceedingly helpful. Of course, one should be careful. One should not be dogmatic and say to every patient, 'Now you paint'. There are people who think: 'Dr Jung's treatment consists in telling his patients to paint', just as formerly they thought: 'He divides them into introverts and extroverts and says "you should live in such and such a way, because you belong to this type or that".' That is certainly not treatment. Each patient is a new problem for the doctor, and he will only be cured of his neurosis if you help him to find his individual way to the solution of his conflicts.

The Chairman:

Ladies and Gentlemen, you have been expressing by your applause something of what you feel about Professor Jung. This is the last time in this group of talks that we will have the honour and pleasure and privilege of hearing Professor Jung. We have only inadequate ways of expressing our thanks to him for these lectures which have been so stimulating, so challenging, which have left us with so many things to think about in the future, things which to all of us, especially those who are practising psychotherapy, are enormously suggestive. I think that is what you meant to do for us, Sir, and that is what you have done. We in this Institute are extremely proud to have had you here talking to us, and all of us, I think, are harbouring the idea that before long you will be back in England to talk to us again and make us think more about these great problems.

NOTES

1   [The case is discussed more fully in 'The Realities of Practical Psychotherapy' (C.W., vol. 16, 2nd edn.), appendix. See also 'Concerning Mandala Symbolism' (C.W., vol. 9, i), pars. 656–659 and figs. 7, 8, and 9, showing mandalas painted by this patient.]
2   [Supra, p. 116.]
3   [This is actually the same case that was discussed supra, pp. 120–21.]
4   [For Jung's later views on this problem, see 'The Psychology of the Transference' (C.W., vol. 16).]
5   *Two Essays* (C. W., vol. 7), pars. 374ff.
6   *Two Essays*, pars. 206ff.
7   'The Role of the Unconscious' (C.W., vol. 10), par. 17.
8   'Wotan'(C.W., vol.10).
9   [Act III, in a speech by Don Juan (Penguin edn., 1952, p. 149).]
10   [Cf. Virgil, *Eclogue V*, 64: 'ipsa sonant arbusta: "deus, deus ille, Menalca!" ' (the very groves ring out: 'A god is he, a god Menalcas!').]
11   See particularly the 'Commentary on *The Secret of the Golden Flower*' (C.W., vol. 13) and 'The Aims of Psychotherapy' (C.W., vol. 16).
12   See *Psychological Types*, Def. 29, and *Two Essays*, pars. 266ff. [Also 'A Study in the Process of Individuation' (C. W., vol. 9, i).]
13   [Cf. *Psychology and Alchemy*, pars. 44, 126, 129, 135, 325ff.]
14   [Cf. *Psychology and Alchemy* (C.W., vol. 12), par. 360.]
15   [This case provided the material for Part II of *Psychology and Alchemy*.]
16   'Traumsymbole des Individuationsprozesses', in the *Eranos-Jahrbuch 1935*. [Now Part II of *Psychology and Alchemy*.]
17   [Cf. 'Commentary on *The Secret of the Golden Flower*' (C.W., vol. 13) and 'Concerning Mandala Symbolism' (C. W., vol. 9, i).]

Appendix: Participants in the Discussions

These sketches, which are necessarily brief, aim to indicate the activity of those who were members of the Institute for Medical Psychology in 1935, when Jung delivered these lectures, and to give selective data on the professional accomplishment and publications of all. Each whose name is marked with an asterisk served as chairman of one of Jung's five lectures.

BAYNES, Helton Godwin (1882–1943), B.A. (Camb.), 1907; M.B., B.Ch., 1912.
Surgeon in Balkan War (Red Cross Mission to Turkey) and First World War. Resident staff, Maudsley Hospital. 1919–22, assistant to C. G. Jung. 1925–26, organized and participated in Jung's expedition to East Africa for research into psychology of native tribes (see Jung, *Memories, Dreams, Reflections*, chap. IX, pt. iii). Translated Jung's *Psychological Types* (1923) and, with Cary F. Baynes, *Contributions to Analytical Psychology* and *Two Essays on Analytical Psychology* (both 1928). Author, *Mythology of the Soul* (1940) and *Germany Possessed* (1941). He was one of the pioneer analytical psychologists and an early representative in England of the Jungian school.

BENDIT, Laurence John, M.A., 1920; D.P.M., 1929; M.D., 1943.
Assistant physician, I.M.P., 1935. Lectured and wrote on psychological and religious subjects, including the years 1961–65 in the United States. Author of various books and articles, including *The Mirror of Life and Death* (1965) and (with Phoebe Bendit) *The Psychic Sense* (1943) and *This World and That* (1950).

BENNET, Edward Armstrong, M.C., M.B., B.Ch., 1925; D.P.M., 1926; M.A., M.D., 1930; D.Sc, 1939.

Physician, I.M.P., 1935. 1942, Brigadier, R.A.M.C.; 1942–45, consultant in psychiatry, India Command and 11th Army Group. Honorary consultant, Tavistock Clinic. Patron, C. G. Jung Institute, Zurich. Author, chapter on psychiatry in *Official History of the Indian Armed Forces 1939–45* (1957); *C. G. Jung* (1961); *What Jung Really Said* (1966).

BION, Wilfred Ruprecht, D.S.O.; B.A. (Oxon.); M.R.C.S.; L.R.C.P. (London), 1930.
Assistant physician, I.M.P., 1935. 1953–59, Director, London Clinic of Psycho-Analysis. 1962–65, President, British Psycho-Analytic Society. Author, *Learning from Experience* (1962); *Elements of Psycho-Analysis* (1963), etc.

BROWNE, Leonard Foster (d. 1960), M.D. (Durham), 1913.
Physician, I.M.P., 1935. Honorary consultant, Tavistock Clinic. 1940–45, Lieutenant-colonel, R.A.M.C.; chief psychiatrist, Eastern Command and London Area. 1949–60, Alderman, County of London; 1957–58, Vice-chairman, London County Council. Author, *Everyday Relationships* (1938).

BRUNTON, Charles, M.A., M.D., Sc.D. (Trinity College, Dublin).
Formerly Senior Lecturer in Physiology at London Hospital Medical College, London University, and at University of Liverpool, where he was also Lecturer in Psychology to Medical Students.

CAMPS, Percy William Leopold (d. 1956), M.B., B.S.; F.R.C.S., 1914–18; R.A.M.C., Malta and France.
Senior surgeon, Teddington Memorial Hospital (Middlesex), which he helped to build.

*CRICHTON-MILLER, Hugh (1877–1959), M.D. (Edinburgh), 1900 and 1902; F.R.C.P. (London), 1939; M.D. (Pavia).
Founder, 1920, Tavistock Clinic. 1946–1959, Vice-President, National Association for Mental Health. 1935, Sir Charles Hastings Lecturer, B.M.A. Patron, C. G. Jung Institute, Zurich. Author, *The New Psychology and the Teacher* (1922); *Psycho-Analysis and Its Derivatives* (1933). Jung wrote the foreword to *Hugh Crichton-Miller, 1877–1959: A Personal Memoir by His Friends and Family* (1961).

DICKS, Henry Victor, M.A., M.D., F.R.C.P. (Cambridge and London).
Assistant medical director, I.M.P., 1935; 1928–51, consultant psychiatrist, Tavistock Clinic. 1940–45, Lieutenant-colonel, R.A.M.C. Adviser in Psychological Warfare, SHAEF. 1946–48, Nuffield Professor of Psychology, Leeds University. 1956, President, Section of Psychiatry, B.M.A. 1966, President, Royal Medical-Psychological Association. 1967, Sussex University,

research in collective psychopathology of Nazi officials. Author, *Clinical Studies in Psychotherapy* (1931); *History of the Tavistock Clinic* (in preparation), etc.

*HADFIELD, James Arthur (1882–), M.A. (Oxon.), 1907; M.B.; Ch.B. (Edinburgh), 1916.
Director of Studies, I.M.P., 1935: in this capacity he invited Jung to England to give the Tavistock Lectures as guest of the Clinic. 1940–45, Lieutenant-colonel, R.A.M.C. Author, *Morals: An Analysis of Character* (1923); *Psychology of Childhood and Adolescence* (1962).

HENDY, Bernard Drummond, M.B.; B.Chir. (Cantab.), 1925.
Physician, I.M.P., 1935. Formerly assistant psychiatrist, De La Pole Hospital, Willerby, Yorkshire.

HOWE, Eric Graham, M.B., B.S. (London), 1927; D.P.M., 1927.
Associate physician, I.M.P., 1935. Author, *Motives and Mechanisms of the Mind* (1930); *The War Dance: A Study of the Psychology of War* (1937); *Mysterious Marriage* (1942); *Cure or Heal* (1965).

LUFF, Mary Constance, M.D. (London), 1931; D.P.M. (Manchester), 1927.
Assistant medical director, I.M.P., 1935. 1940–45, Major, R.A.M.C. Now retired in Jamaica (W.I.).

MACKENZIE, Marion Enid Townsend, M.B.; B.S. (London), 1931.
Consultant, psychiatric department for children and parents, Tavistock Clinic. Associate member, British Psycho-Analytical Society. Author, papers in journals on public health.

*MILLER, Emanuel (1893–), M.A., D.P.M. (Cantab.); F.R.C.P. (London), 1946.
Physician, I.M.P., 1935. 1940–45, Lieutenant-colonel, R.A.M.C.; psychiatrist to directorate of Medical Research and Statistics, 1958. From 1948, joint editor, *British Journal of Criminology*. Author, *Modern Psychotherapy* (1931); *Neuroses in War* (editor, 1940); *Foundations of Child Psychiatry* (in press).

*REES, John Rawlings (1890–), C.B.E. (Military Div.); M.A., M.D. (Cantab.), D.P.M., 1920; F.R.C.P., 1944.
Medical Director, I.M.P., 1935. 1939–45, Brigadier, R.A.M.C.; 1944–45, honorary consulting psychiatrist to Army. 1948–49, President, World Federation of Mental Health; 1949–62, its director, and 1962, its honorary president. Honorary member of professional associations in many countries; numerous lectureships and awards. Author, *The Case of Rudolf Hess* (editor, 1947); *Mental Health and the Offender* (1949).

Ross, Thomas Arthur (d. 1941), M.D. (Edinburgh), 1901; F.R.C.P. (London and Edinburgh).
Resident physician and surgeon, Royal Infirmary, Edinburgh. Author, The Common Neuroses (1923); An Introduction to Analytical Psychotherapy (1932).

Strauss, Eric Benjamin (d. 1961), M.A. (Oxon.), 1930; F.R.C.P. (London), 1939; Hon. D.Sc. (Frankfurt).
Assistant physician, I.M.P., 1935. Croonian Lecturer, R.C.P., 1952. Author, Recent Advances in Neurology (1929), with W. R. Brain (later Lord Brain); Psychiatry in the ModernWorld (1958); translator, E. Kretschmer's Text Book of Medical Psychology (1934).

Suttie, Ian Dishart (d. 1935), F.R.F.P.S., 1920; M.D., 1931 (all Glasgow).
Physician, I.M.P., 1935. 1935, assistant physician, Glasgow Royal Asylum. Author, The Origins of Love and Hate (1935).

*Wright, Maurice Beresford (d. 1951), O.B.E.; M.D. (Edinburgh), 1906.
Physician, I.M.P., 1935. Neurological specialist to Ministry of Pensions.

Yellowlees, David, M.B.,Ch.B.
Formerly consulting psychiatrist, Glasgow Western Infirmary, and Medical Director of the Lansdowne Clinic for Functional Nervous Disorders, Glasgow. Author, Psychology's Defence of the Faith (1930).

LIST OF WORKS CITED

ADLER, Gerhard – *Entdeckung der Seele; Von Sigmund Freud und Alfred Adler zu C. G. Jung.* Zurich, 1934.

BOURGET, Paul – *L'Étape.* 1902.

BUDGE, E. A. Wallis – *Egyptian Literature.* Vol. I, *Legends of the Gods.* (Books on Egypt and Chaldea, 32.) London, 1912.

DAVIE, T. M. – 'Comments upon a Case of "Periventricular Epilepsy"', *British Medical Journal* (London), 1935, vol. II, 293–297 (no. 3893, Aug. 17).

DIETERICH, Albrecht – *Eine Mithrasliturgie.* Leipzig, 1903; 2nd edn., 1910. Translated by G. R. S. Mead: *A Mithriac Ritual.* London and Benares, 1907.

DUNS SCOTUS – *Super universalibus Porphyrii.*

EVANS-WENTZ, W. Y. – *The Tibetan Book of the Dead.* London, 1927; 3rd edn., with commentary by Jung, 1957.

FOUCART, P. F. – *Les Mystères d'Eleusis.* Paris, 1914.

FREUNDLICH, Jakob – Article in *Deutsches Archiv für klinische Medizin* (Berlin), 177:4 (1934), 449–57.

GRENFELL, Bernard P., and Arthur S. HUNT (eds. and trans.) *New Sayings of Jesus and Fragment of a Lost Gospel.* London, 1904.

GUILLAUME de DIGUILEVILLE – *Le Pèlerinage de la vie humaine. Le Pèlerinage de l'âme. Le Pèlerinage de Jésus Christ.* In: JOSEPH DELACOTTE. *Guillaume de Diguileville . . . Trois romans poèmes du XIVe siècle.* Paris, 1932.

HARRISON, Jane E. – *Prolegomena to the Study of Greek Religion.* 3rd edn., Cambridge, 1922.

HERMAS – *The Shepherd.* In: KIRSOPP LAKE (ed. and trans.) *The Apostolic Fathers,* vol. II (Loeb Classical Library). London and New York, 1913.

HERODOTUS – *The Histories.* Translated by Aubrey de Selincourt (Penguin Classics). Harmondsworth, 1954.

HEYER, G. R. – *The Organism of the Mind.* Translated by E. and C. Paul. London, 1933.

HUBERT, Henri, and Marcel MAUSS – *Mélanges d'histoire des religions*. Paris, 1909.

I Ching, or Book of Changes, The. – Richard Wilhelm's translation, rendered into English by Cary F. Baynes. With a foreword by C. G. Jung. New York and London, 1950. 2 vols. 3rd edn. in 1 vol., 1968.

JACOBI, Jolande – *Complex/Archetype/Symbol in the Psychology of C. G. Jung*. Translated by Ralph Manheim. With a foreword by C. G. Jung. New York and London, 1959.

JOSEPHUS, Flavius – *The Jewish War*. (Loeb Classical Library *Josephus*, II, III.) Cambridge, Mass., and London, 1927. 2 vols.

JUNG, C. G. – For writings cited in the Collected Works, see the list at the end of this volume. Other editions cited: *The Integration of the Personality*. Translated by Stanley Dell. New York, 1939; London, 1940. *Psychological Types*. Translated by H. G. Baynes. London and New York, 1923. *Psychologie und Alchemie*. Zurich, 1944; 2nd rev. edn., 1952. *Studies in Word Association*. Translated by M. D. Eder. London, 1918; New York, 1919.

KANT, Immanuel – *Anthropologie in pragmatischer Hinsicht*. 1798.

KRANEFELDT, W. M. – *Secret Ways of the Mind*. Translated by Ralph Eaton. London, 1932.

LE BON, Gustave. – *The Crowd: A Study of the Popular Mind*. London, 1897. (Trans. from *Psychologie des foules*, 1895.)

LÉVY-BRUHL, Lucien – *How Natives Think*. Translated by Lilian A. Clare. London, 1926.

SHAW, George Bernard – *Man and Superman: A Comedy and A Philosophy*. London, 1903. (Penguin edn., 1952, as cited on p.135.)

SOPHOCLES – 'Life of Sophocles', in: *Sophoclis Fabulae*. Edited by A. C. Pearson. Oxford, 1924.

THOMPSON, R. Campbell (trans.) – *The Epic of Gilgamish*. London, 1928.

WILLCOX, A. R. – *The Rock Art of South Africa*. Johannesburg, 1963.

INDEX

Made in the USA
Las Vegas, NV
02 November 2021